eed Brown's 1841 Journey

AMERICA THROUGH THE EYES OF A VERMONT YANKEE

RICHARD H. ALLEN

191 Bank Street
Burlington, Vermont 05401

Onion River Press
191 Bank Street
Burlington, VT 05401

Names: Allen, Richard H., author.
Title: Reed Brown's 1841 journey : America through the eyes of a Vermont Yankee / Richard H. Allen.
Description: Includes index and bibliographical references. | Burlington, VT: Onion River Press, 2018.
Identifiers: LCCN 2018910017 | ISBN 978-1-949066-09-8
Subjects: LCSH: Brown, Reed Briggs--Travel--United States. | United States--Description and travel. | United States--History--19th century. | Travel writing--History--19th century. | United States--Social life and customs--19th century. | BISAC HISTORY / United States / 19th Century | TRAVEL / Special Interest / General
Classification: LCC E166 .A42 2018 | DDC 973.5--dc23

Printed in the United States of America

Front cover illustration: Jacob Abbott, *Marco Paul's Voyages & Travels*

(New York: Harper & Brothers, c. 1852).

Design & Production by Sue Storey Design & Illustration

Sponsored and partially financed
by the Williston Historical Society
PO Box 995
Williston, Vermont 05495

Reed Brown's 1841 Journey

AMERICA THROUGH THE EYES OF A VERMONT YANKEE

To librarians, past and present,
who have been so helpful
with the historical research
through the years.

$\mathscr{C}$ONTENTS

$\mathcal{I}$NTRODUCTION

$\mathcal{I}$n 1979, Lorraine Brown of Maumee, Ohio, visited Williston, Vermont, to learn more about the birthplace of her great-grandfather, Reed Briggs Brown.[1] A few years later, she presented a journal written by Reed Brown to the Williston Historical Society. Because of her generous donation, a rare and fascinating pre-Civil War primary source has been preserved, allowing us a glimpse into one man's view of his world.

Part of Reed Brown's journal is a record of his 1841 excursion to New York City, Washington, D.C., and Ohio. He took his trip for both business and personal reasons. He was a blacksmith, and he had designed an improved set of carriage springs that needed a patent. His other concern was his brother, Nathaniel, who was in jail in Ravenna, Ohio, for the burglary of a grocery store in Akron.

On September 22, 1841, Reed set out on a two-month odyssey to accomplish his goals. Like many fellow Americans, Reed took advantage of the country's burgeoning transportation system, including roads, canals, and rails. The success of the Erie Canal led to "canal fever" and a rush to build upon the economic boost experienced in New York State. The National Road crossed the Appalachian Mountains and provided a land route for migrants and travelers. A growing network of railroads connected the major cities of the United States.

Reed noted the dangers and difficulties, as well as some of the pleasures, of travel in that time. He wrote about his triumphs, setbacks, and successful return to Vermont. He experienced a steamboat explosion, a rail car derailment, hours of a bone-jarring stagecoach ride, delayed canal boat passage, seasickness, blistered feet, exhaustion, and fleas. His personality and interests show through in his comments about the land, the crops, the people, and the buildings he saw, as well as social issues such as temperance. His actions reveal a caring soul, an inquisitive mind, and a bent for social engagement. He was not a fluid writer, but his story comes across in a clear and engaging manner.

But this is more than one man's story. In some respects, Reed's journey mirrored what the rapidly maturing country was experiencing on a larger scale. Like many Americans who were forsaking rural for urban life, Reed left small-town Vermont, and within days he had seen several of the large cities on the East Coast. It was a fast-forward view of the future urbanization of the country and the workings of its developing government. Because of his rural background, he critiqued the agricultural practices he observed throughout his journey, but he was also observing broader historical trends. He came in contact with people of different ethnic groups, foreshadowing a development that would play a major role in the nation's growth through the second half of the 19th century and into the 20th century. In addition, his experience with the patent process provides some insights into one of early America's truly successful government programs.

The second part of Reed's journey mirrored the westward migration of portions of the nation's population, moving from the settled eastern seaboard to the interior of the country. He gained firsthand knowledge about what drew people away from Vermont to places like Ohio and what sent some back to their home state. As people from Vermont migrated to the western states and urban areas of the east, the state's population growth was minimal, and concerns were voiced about its future because some of its best people were leaving for opportunities elsewhere. Reed gained a new appreciation for what he had in Vermont. In the end, he did not migrate. Satisfied with his lot in Vermont, he and his wife Electa raised their family there, providing for them by farming and later with a business.

Besides common folk like Reed Brown, many others were traveling across the land. It took free time and economic independence, but those who were so blessed, particularly English men and women, loved to tour the United States. They explored big cities such as Boston, New York, Washington, and Cincinnati, frequently with a side trip to see Niagara Falls. Literate sojourners produced an estimated 200 travelogues between 1815 and 1860.[2] Some visitors from the "mother country" were curious about the American experiment in democracy; others were interested in the people who were settling along the travel routes, especially as they headed west to Ohio, Michigan, and Illinois. The landscape also captivated sightseers. They often left erudite records of their trips in the form of letters to newspapers and books.

English travelers' perspectives on American transportation affected their experiences. They frequently expressed condescension toward Americans in their description of rough roads, slow canal boats, and ill-mannered citizens. For example, after arriving in 1827 from England and living in the United States for several years, Frances Milton Trollope wrote *Domestic Manners of the Americans*. She was appalled by most of what she observed and experienced. Though her book became a bestseller, Americans railed soundly against it. Charles Dickens' 1842 travels in the United

States yielded *American Notes,* in which he, like Trollope, criticized slavery, the seemingly class-less society, and boorish manners. In addition, his descriptions of transportation illustrated the challenges of getting around at that time.

Dickens had this to say about Trollope: "I am convinced that there is no writer who has so well and so accurately (I need not add entertainingly) described America."[3] Trollope and Dickens, as well as Nathaniel Hawthorne and several other less well-known writers, have left us with detailed descriptions of the trials and rewards of touring in the United States before the Civil War.

Frances Trollope, 1832, by Auguste Hervieu. Wikimedia Commons, public domain.

Unlike these famous writers, Reed Brown's experiences were recorded with no thought of publication in a journal 8 by 12½ inches, which encompass about 160 pages of business transactions and an account of the journey. It spans the period from December 26, 1837, to 1865 intermittently. Many of the pages are covered with items that were added later — greeting cards, post cards, and images cut from books and magazines — turning parts of the journal into a scrapbook. The ephemera can interfere with deciphering the entries. Since the trip pages are generally spared from being covered by miscellaneous material, someone thought the story of Reed's journey was worth saving and perhaps reproducing someday. The pages describing the trip are written in ink, quite readable, with acceptable penmanship, variable spelling, and simple vocabulary. However, Reed lists "pencil points" among his expenses, and it is reasonable to question why he would take a large account book containing several years of business records along on his journey. It is possible that he recorded on the road in a smaller notebook in pencil and transferred the story to the journal in ink after his return to Vermont. Also, the steady hand and even penmanship suggest that it was written at a desk in an unhurried fashion. Further evidence of this sequence is suggested by his insertion of "1842" in some of the entries, in place of "1841." This could indicate that he was writing in the larger journal after the New Year and was having trouble

Charles Dickens, 1839, by Daniel Maclise. Wikimedia Commons, public domain.

Reed Brown's first entry in his journal recounting the start of his journey in the fall of 1841. Williston Historical Society, Williston, Vermont.

keeping the correct year in mind.

The journal entries, transcribed in italics and in chronological order, have been researched and annotated to create a historical context for Reed's experiences. The transcript provided here has retained the original spelling as much as possible, though capital letters and some punctuation have been added to make reading easier.

Reed did not follow the traditional format of recording the date and limiting his entry to what happened on that day. Often the day-to-day action carries over from one page to another under the same date, and his travel at night complicates matters. Also, because Reed had trouble keeping track of the dates and some of the days, there are detectable mistakes. Where these occur, the correct days and dates have been inserted in brackets. Several times he skips a day. Where he notes the place and date on the top of a journal page, they are inserted in the text.

After several years of reviewing the material in the Williston Historical Society archives, I was intrigued by Reed's journal and the story it told. Obviously, he felt that his trip was important enough to record, and his descendants felt the same way, as it was passed on from generation to generation. Too often history is written by and about the famous movers and shakers. This journal gives us a small chance to even out the balance by exploring a common man's story. When combined with the observations of other writers, Reed's journal provides a fascinating look into antebellum life in America through the eyes of a Vermont Yankee stepping into the unfamiliar territory of big cities, different landscapes, and people of other races and occupations. It also offers a firsthand view of the difficulty of travel in the United States at that time, both through Reed's experiences and those of others making their way across a dynamic, expanding country.

— *Richard Allen*
Essex, Vermont
August 2018

* * * * * * * *

CHAPTER 1

Up Lake Champlain and Down the Hudson River

*I*n late September 1841, 31-year-old Reed Briggs Brown left his wife Electa and their three children, Polly Ann, age 8, Jackson, soon to be 7, and Bertram, age 1, and started on the adventure of a lifetime. Gone from home for 57 days, he covered about 2,150 miles. Combining business, sightseeing, and a personal quest, Reed joined many in the antebellum age who explored the country and then produced a travelogue.

Essex Sept 24ᵗʰ [22ⁿᵈ] 1841

Wensday Sept 24ᵗʰ [22ⁿᵈ] 1841. Start for the cittey of Washington at 4 oclock P.M. Got to Burlington after gowing to Williston at dusk, toke passage on the Steamboat Burlington (Capt. Shirman). Paid for Pasage to Whitehall $2.50. For six crackers, one apple, 7 cents.

Vewed a modelle of a 74 gunship made of Ivery and cost five hundred dollars. It was given to Capt Shirmay by New York Cittey. It is a grate curiosity. It is compleatley fitted out with canons and even maned with men made of Plaster peris.

Reed began in Essex, Vermont, where he was currently living, near the intersection of what are now Weed and Naylor roads. He either walked to Williston, crossing the Winooski River on a ferry, or took a horse to his father's house there, and then continued on foot to Burlington, probably on the Winooski Turnpike.

Reed boarded the steamer *Burlington* in Burlington harbor. Before railroads, these boats and others were the major form of transportation for people and goods on Lake Champlain. At that time, Burlington, with a population of 4,271, was the state's largest city. "By 1840 [the] harbor area boasted a lighthouse, three thriving commercial wharves, and an annual trade estimated at over one million dollars."[1] The opening of the Champlain Canal in 1823 provided a connection from Lake Champlain to the Hudson River and greater markets for Vermont products, giving a strong boost to Burlington's economy.

Reed sailed with the most famous steamer captain on the lake, Richard Sherman. Sherman was born into a nautical family; his father was a steamboat captain. He spent some time on the Hudson River, and returned to Lake Champlain in 1837. Famous for his fastidious attention to passenger comfort, at one time Sherman "detailed a hand with a mop to follow round a well-dressed tobacco chewer among his passengers, and swab up each discharge as soon as it lighted on his clean deck."[2] The discipline and beauty of his ship "[made] the *Burlington* celebrated as the 'paragon of steamers' both in America and Europe."[3]

The ivory ship model of a 74-gun frigate mentioned by Reed was perhaps a tribute to the bravery Sherman displayed when he saved lives from the burning *Phoenix*, near Providence Island on Lake Champlain, in September 1819. With his father sick at home, the 21-year-old Sherman had assumed command of the vessel and directed the rescue effort.[4] Receiving a model of such a large and important ship was quite an honor.[5]

As Reed Brown was traveling in the fall of 1841, a much more famous person was planning a tour of the United States. Charles Dickens, only 29 years old, was already celebrated for the publication of *The Pickwick Papers*, *Oliver Twist*, and *Nicholas Nickleby*. Dickens' tour started in January and lasted until June 1842. He later produced *American Notes*, which detailed his travels and observations on the American experiment with democracy.

Captain Richard Sherman. Ogden Ross, *The Steamboats of Lake Champlain, 1809 to 1930* (Rutland, VT: Vermont Heritage Press, 1997).

Near the end of his tour, Dickens traveled up Lake Champlain, on the same steamer that Reed used in September, under the charge of Captain Sherman. He remarked:

[T]he *Burlington* is a perfectly exquisite achievement of neatness, elegance, and order. The decks are drawing rooms; the cabins are boudoirs, choicely furnished and adorned with prints, pictures, and musical instruments; every nook and corner of the vessel is a perfect curiosity of graceful comfort and beautiful contrivance. Captain Sherman, her commander, to whose ingenuity and excellent taste these results are solely attributable, has bravely and worthily distinguished himself on more than one trying occasion; not least among them in having the moral courage to carry British troops at a time (during the Canadian rebellion) when no other conveyance was open to

The steamer *Burlington* was built at Shelburne Harbor in 1837 for $75,000. The 190-foot-long boat had a displacement of 405 tons and could travel at 15 miles per hour. Special Collections, Bailey/Howe Library, University of Vermont.

them. He and his vessel are held in universal respect, both by his own countrymen and ours; and no man ever enjoyed the popular esteem, who, in his sphere of action, won and wore it better than this gentleman.[6]

Thursday Morning Sept 25 [23]—1841

Got up at 3 oclock. Verry foggey and coald Sunrise. Got to the narrows whare thay have to gow ashore with Ropes to ceap off of the shores. Caled the fidlers Elbo. 6 oclock got to Whitehall. Pleasant plase, but is verry rockey. Got Breckfast at a privett house 25 cents. Two News papers 12½ cents, and sent them home. Three sheets paper. 3 cents.

Charles Dickens had a similar experience in Fiddler's Elbow, where, he said, "steamboats lie by for some hours in the night, in consequence of the lake becoming very narrow at that part of the journey, and difficult of navigation in the dark. Its width is so contracted at one point, indeed, that they are obliged to warp round by means of a rope."[7] To "warp round" is to maneuver a boat with a line attached to a fixed point.

Though Reed thought Whitehall rather pleasant, an earlier traveler disagreed: "[I]ts appearance was anything but favorable…the country was rough and wild in every direction…. The village seemed to have been thrown by some convulsion into a dreary mountain pass, of the most forbidding description." At the same time, the town's strategic location was recognized: "[T]he town looked like a smart business place as it must necessarily be from its position, standing at the junction of the Champlain canal and the lake, and in a chasm through which all Northern travelers not

Northern view of Whitehall.

Whitehall. Wood Creek and the Champlain Canal appear in the center. John
W. Barber and Henry Howe, *Historical Collections of the State of New York* (New
York: S. Tuttle, 1846).

taking the route of Lake George must pass, and at which they must stop."[8]

Reed's notation that two newspapers cost 12½ cents reflects the origins of coinage in circulation in the 1840s. The Spanish dollar, the basis of the American dollar, was a legitimate coin in the United States until 1857. When smaller amounts were called for, the dollar was divided into eighths, or "pieces of eight," each worth 12½ cents, called a bit.[9]

Met Tiras Hall from St Lawrance Co Ny. Showed him the springs; he wants the Patent for st co. Tride to get stage Pasage, but could not. Hevey loaded. Took Pasage in Packett North America *for Troy, paid for Pasage $2. To sand Hill Rather Poor country. Rather mountainous from Fort Ann to Fort Miller. Rather better land and verry level.*

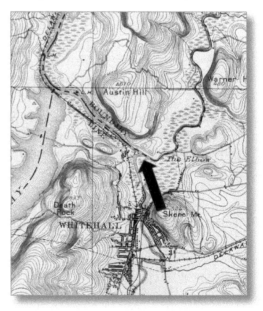

Fiddler's Elbow (arrow) north of Whitehall on the 1902 topographical map. "The ride to Whitehall is a pleasant, and would be a very short one, were it not for the vexatious navigation of the short crooks or angles in the narrow upper end of the lake called 'Fiddler's Elbow.'"[10]

Reed met with Tiras Hall of St. Lawrence County in northern New York to make a contact for future sales of his improved carriage springs. Later, in 1842, Reed closed several deals on his patent in that region (see the epilogue). What Reed showed Mr. Hall was probably his model of the carriage springs. Along with drawings and a written description, the other requirement for receiving a patent was to submit a working model no larger than a cubic foot.

The overloaded stagecoach forced Reed to book passage on the packet boat *North America* headed to Troy, New York, by the Champlain Canal. Packet boats, named for their original cargo of mail packets, were designed to carry passengers exclusively on a regular schedule. Because they had right of way over freight boats, these boats reduced travel time. For example, fast horse relays pulled Peter Comstock's boats from Whitehall to Troy in twenty-four hours.[11]

Travel on a packet was certainly a step down from the luxurious steamer *Burlington.* Packets were narrow, about $13\frac{1}{2}$ feet wide and 78 feet long, with a small deck in the bow and one in the stern that gave room for the captain to operate a tiller. Most passengers stayed in a single-room cabin stretching almost the entire length of the boat. People could also ride on the roof but had to look out for low bridges that could knock them into the canal. The central window-lined cabin served as a passenger compartment, dining area, and sleeping quarters, which were divided by curtains. Cramped and noisy, packets provided efficient, but rudimentary, accommodations.[12]

THE PACKET BOAT.

A packet boat on the Erie Canal. Jacob Abbott, *Marco Paul's Voyages & Travels* (New York: Harper & Brothers, c. 1852).

The Champlain Canal, completed in 1823, ran between Waterford, New York, and Whitehall, connecting Lake Champlain to the Hudson River and points south. Most of the route was a constructed channel of $46\frac{1}{2}$ miles, including locks to overcome an elevation change, plus 11 miles of the Hudson River, and $6\frac{1}{2}$ miles of Wood Creek near Whitehall. Located strategically between the canal and the lake, Whitehall boomed. Heavy loads of iron ore and lumber were shipped with greater ease, and the economies of New York lake towns such as Ticonderoga, Port Henry, and Port Kent also benefited.[13]

The Champlain Canal was challenged early in 1835 by the railroad, which headed north via the Rensselaer & Saratoga line, and later the Saratoga & White-hall in 1848. Rail shipment was faster and available year-round. But the canal remained attractive to small operators who could own their boats and ship their goods directly.[14]

Near Ft Miller is the plase Gen Begoin [Burgoyne] surrendered his armey to the Americans. It was on the bank of the River. Slep on a shelf, Rested well.

In 1777, British commander "Gentleman Johnny" Burgoyne marched from Canada along Lake Champlain with the intent of isolating New England from the rest of the colonies during the Revolutionary War. A contingent was defeated at the Battle of Bennington and other troops delayed near Fort Anne (between Whitehall and Glens Falls).[15] Burgoyne eventually surrendered at Saratoga on October 17. This defeat is often cited as a turning point of the war. Reed's mention of this in his journal is indicative that the Revolution was still recent history for some, and veterans, like Reed's 83-year-old grandfather, John Brown Sr. (1758-1855), were still alive to keep it so.

Traveler "R.V.M." supplied a more eloquent description of the route in 1848. "The most interesting scenery to me on the 'Packet Boat' along the Champlain Canal is beyond Glen's Falls then by Fort Miller to Stillwater. The fine view of 'North River' [Hudson River], and the adjacent scenery among the hills, where occurred so many struggles and stirring events of the Revolution, and within sight of the battle ground of Saratoga, renders this part of the route an object of interest to the traveler."[16]

Remains of the Champlain Canal in Waterford, New York, May 9, 2017. Photograph by the author.

Friday Morning Sept 26 [24]—1841

Got up at 5 oclock and found that I was at west Troy. Paid for blacking boots 10 cents, for breckfast 25 cents. Steam boat redey to start for Albany, so that I had no time to vew the Plase. Pade for pasage to Albany, 12½ cents, verry Pleasant country. Troy is on a rather low pease of land. Albany is sittuated much like Burlington VT, but a grate deal larger. Diner 6 cents, supper 37 cents.

Located on the west bank of the Hudson River, West Troy was incorporated as a village in 1836. It was later included in the city of Watervliet.[17]

Dinner was the midday meal equivalent to lunch, and supper was in the evening. Reed's reference point for comparing cities was Burlington, Vermont. But Albany was much busier; with an 1840 population of 33,721, it was the ninth largest city in the country. At the eastern terminus of the Erie Canal, the local economy was supported by the shipment of goods from the canal south to New York City, as well as west in the opposite direction. The great number of boats created a scene of controlled chaos as freight was off-loaded from river barges to canal boats and vice versa. Steamers added noise and commotion to the scene. Besides shipping, "lumber, stove manufacturing, and brewing were Albany's major industries during the 1840s."[18]

From Troy to Albany I past 54 boats. At Albany, the River was mostley covered with Boats.

Reed Brown was now traveling on the 315-mile-long Hudson River, which originates in the Adirondack Mountains of New York and flows south to empty into the Atlantic Ocean at New York City. The river played an instrumental role in the settlement of the colonies and the Revolutionary War, and to this day it remains important as a transportation route connected to the New York State Canal System.

Took steam Boat Albany *for N york Friday Morning at 7 oclock. Paid passage $1.50. 9 oclock comenced Raining. Past quite anumber Pleasant vileidges. Land ginerly verry good. Had conversation with a man that had ben to Washington to obtain a patent on a screw plate. Tells me to cal on Doct Jones and he help me to get A patent.*

$$4.97 + 2.41 = 7.38$$

A screw plate is a threaded metal plate with holes to create threads on a screw.

The steamer *Albany* was built in 1826 in Philadelphia and put on the New York City-to-Albany route in April 1827. To shorten the travel time between the cities, builders modified the vessel by increasing its length and width to give it sharper lines. The original 12-hour passage was thus reduced to eight and a half.[19]

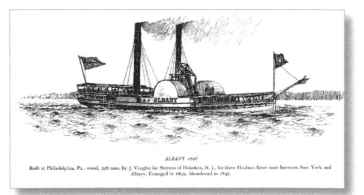

ALBANY 1826

Built at Philadelphia, Pa., wood, 398 tons, by J. Vaughn for Stevens of Hoboken, N. J., for their Hudson River route between New York and Albany. Enlarged in 1839. Abandoned in 1843.

Steamer *Albany*. Illustration by Samuel Ward Stanton, maritime artist (1860-1912). *Hudson River Steamboats* (Meriden, CT: Meriden Gravure Co., 1964). Courtesy of Allynne Lange, curator, Hudson River Maritime Museum, Kingston, New York.

Friday Noon Sept 26 [24]

The main rod that cares [carries] the steam boat broke And stove the Pilots cabin all to peaces. And throde the two Pilots on to the lower deck and throde some of the peaces as much as twenty rods. And how we all acape with out being hurt is more than I can tell. There was about 150 basengers. Some ware for Joumping over borde and would if thay had not ben stop by the others. The caus was inconcequenes of a poor weld. It had been 5 years. There was quite anoiz when it broke. Stop Raining, but we have ben 3 hours ancored in the river. Rather lonsom, but I got as good a chance as the others. The Capt sais the damage is 15 or 20 thousand dollars.

Reed and his fellow passengers were lucky to have survived this incident. Steamboats suffered terrible accidents and explosions on the Hudson River, the Mississippi, the Ohio, and other waters. Captains would sometimes race with another boat, which could overtax the boilers and result in an explosion and fire. Cutthroat competition between companies promoted such dangerous races, as did less risky ploys such as directing passengers off a train to mistakenly board the wrong boat.[20]

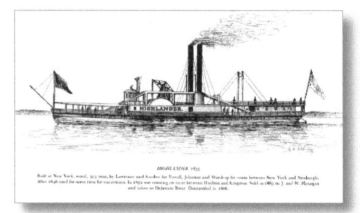

Steamer *Highlander.* Illustration by Samuel Ward Stanton, maritime artist (1860-1912). *Hudson River Steamboats,* (Meriden, CT: Meriden Gravure Co., 1964). Courtesy of Allynne Lange, curator, Hudson River Maritime Museum, Kingston, New York.

The *New York Tribune* gave an outsider's perspective on the accident Reed experienced: "As the steamboat *Albany* was coming down yesterday afternoon, her connecting rod parted and let the pisten down with great force, also bursting the cylinder. Part of the machinery tore up the deck near the pilot house, the Pilot Engineer and one of the passengers narrowly escaping."[21]

Stuck on a disabled boat and awaiting rescue, Reed and his fellow passengers must have been relieved when another boat, the *Highlander,* pulled in sight and promised to take them on from the accident location about three miles above Newburgh.

The *Highlander,* one of the speediest and most modern boats on the river at that time, was constructed in 1835 in New York City by Lawrence and Sneden. Its regular run was between the city and Newburgh, also serving Caldwell's, West Point, and Cold Springs, all on the Hudson River.

But even the passage on the *Highlander* proved challenging, crowded, and odiferous.

5 oclock. Comes On other boat to take us on to N. York. Rather small and loded with cattle, sheep, hogs & horces and fresh pork. There is so meney of us that we cant sit down. Have to hang up amonst the cattle and the horses. Rainey---11 oclock at nite, land at N. York cittey.

The *Albany* was repaired and back on its route the next spring, leaving the steamboat pier for Albany from the foot of Barclay Street each Monday, Wednesday, and Friday. Under the guidance of Captain J. G. Jenkins, travelers were assured that it was a "low-pressure" steamboat.[22]

The explosion on the *Albany* certainly rattled Reed's nerves and probably made him question whether he should continue his journey. He would face new challenges in the largest city in the country, New York.

. . . .

*C*HAPTER 2

NEW YORK CITY

*A*fter the nerve-wracking explosion on the steamboat on the Hudson River, Reed needed some well-deserved rest.

Gow to A temperance house. Cant get Lodgein. In company of Mr. Waterbury, Gow to the Merchants Hotell. Git supper 50 cents. Poor nites Rest on act [account] *of fleas.*

Landing at Warren Street, Reed walked about nine blocks to the Merchants' Hotel at 41 Courtlandt Street.

When Charles Wyckoff opened the five-story Merchants' Hotel in 1840, he claimed it was larger than his previous house and "was fitted up with sitting parlors in modern style, and sixty furnished bedrooms." He hoped his old customers would continue their patronage of "the new establishment."[1]

1857 receipt for the Merchants' Hotel, New York City. The Delaware County Historical Association Archives, Delhi, New York.

The Merchants' Hotel was not Reed's first choice for accommodations. He much preferred a temperance house where he could avoid the noise, profane language, and disturbances of people drinking alcohol. He wasn't going to have much luck in finding such an establishment in New York City, for an 1845 guide to the city had advertisements for 17 hotels, only three of which were temperance houses. One promoted itself for "All friends of Temperance desiring a quiet home, and freedom from the fumes of Alcohol and Tobacco." Evidently the availability of strong drink was preferred by most travelers and also by innkeepers who realized an increase in profits from the sales.[2]

The temperance movement, one of the largest and most successful social reform efforts of the early 19th century, intended to reduce the amount of damage to society, especially families and children, brought on by the overindulgence in drink. Upper-class residents of New York City in the mid-1820s worried that alcohol was "eroding ambition, dissipating wealth, and spawning domestic violence."[3] Temperance societies flourished across the country — about 5,000 were operating by 1834 — and successfully decreased alcohol use. "After peaking in 1830 (at roughly five gallons per capita annually), alcohol consumption sharply declined by the 1840s (to under two)."[4]

A pen is offered to the husband so that he can sign the temperance pledge on the table. "This is to certify that ... was duly elected a member of the above society on the ... day of ... 184-, and the pledge having been in due form administered to him he signed the same." Thomas S. Sinclair, lithographer, published by James Porter, c. 1841. Library of Congress.

New York Cittey Sept 27 [25]—1841

Saterday Morning sept 27 [25] — 1841. In New York and it rains verry hard. Got up and went down 5 pare [of] stares. Got in to a cap [cab]. Paid cab man $1.00. Went to the collectors office to see if I could not git my patent with out gowing to Washington; but he told me I had better gow to Washington.

Reed had good reason to believe that a collector — known as a collector of customs — could help him obtain a patent. This federal official "raised revenues and controlled shipping, placed duties on imports, prevented smuggling and enforced the laws regulating exports and imports," and was also empowered to assist in the patent process.[5]

A devastating fire hit the Patent Office in Washington, D.C., on December 15,

1836, destroying all the records and models of the ten thousand patents kept there. To recreate the records, the Patent Office encouraged those who were affected by the fire to forward whatever copies of their patents they had retained, and duplicate models. Given the disarray in the patent process caused by the fire, models could be forwarded by the customs collectors. Reed might have asked to have his patent application sent through the collector and been turned down because he was missing the technical drawings, as he would later learn in Washington. If Reed had sought this service in New York City, it raises the question: Did he go to the collector based in Burlington, Vermont, before his trip and seek the same?[6]

Reed had some firsthand knowledge of the patent process from an acquaintance and person with whom he did business, Hiram Phelps. Phelps, born in Connecticut in 1801, lived most of his life in Williston, Vermont, Reed's original hometown. Like Reed, he started out as a blacksmith. Phelps also held a patent, granted June 21, 1835 (number 8923X), for a butter churn.[7] The drawings and records for the Phelps churn were most certainly destroyed in the 1836 Patent Office fire. Reed knew this as he went through the patent application process; indeed, he probably made a promise to himself and his family that the papers for his carriage springs patent would be properly filed and duplicated.

The Patent Act of 1836 implemented several significant reforms. The Patent Office gained some independence from the secretary of state's office and was now headed by a commissioner. Before 1836, patents were automatically given without any professional evaluation done by knowledgeable examiners (except from 1790 to 1793). This led to patent piracy and "fraudulent sales of patent licenses." That changed with the hiring of more staff trained to do a proper assessment of each application.[8] Information on approved patents was made public so that applicants could gain a better understanding of the uniqueness of their ideas and their chances of receiving a patent.

Reed was not alone in this in-person approach to applying for a patent. Patent Office historian Kenneth W. Dobyns states that, "It was common practice for an in-

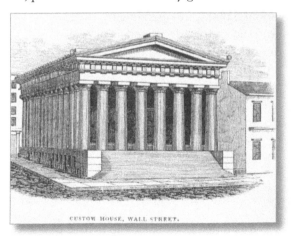

CUSTOM HOUSE, WALL STREET.

The Custom House from the Ruggles 1846 guide to New York City. Started in 1834 and completed in May of 1841, this building designed by John Frazee mimics the Parthenon of ancient Greece. It is now the Federal Hall National Memorial (26 Wall Street), built on the site of Federal Hall (1700-1812), where George Washington was inaugurated as the first president.

ventor to travel to Washington from a great distance, expecting to apply for a patent and carry the issued patent home with him."[9] Given the revised application process with its additional requirements, the fees, and the fact that only two-fifths of the applications submitted resulted in an approved patent, Reed was advised by more than one person to continue to Washington to submit a technical drawing, a model, and to make the payments.

> *Took Rail Rode to the Peano Factory to see Wales F. Grow. Pasage 12½ cents. Grow at 3rd avenue 22 st. 10 clock. Stop raining. Find Grow verry sick. Cant leve the house.*

By 1838, New York had a rail line that ran from City Hall to Harlem. A small steam engine served in the northern parts of the city and horses in the more compactly settled lower Manhattan, as steam engines were not deemed fully safe.[10] "A railroad yonder, see, where two stout horses trot along, drawing a score or two of people and a great wooden ark, with ease," wrote Charles Dickens.[11]

Vermonter Wales French Grow (1806-1878) was probably part of Reed Brown's extended family; the exact relationship is unknown.[12] Grow was involved in the manufacture of pianos.[13]

> *Gow back to the Park and cant find the Hotell. Pay cabman to carray me to the hotell. 25 cents. Had to by an umberella, $1.50. 11 oclock. Wrote to Nathaniel and Mailed two papers for home, cost 10 cents. Gow to the Post Office, but cant find the way back.*

Oh, the woes of a country dweller dealing with city life! Reed got lost twice but was resourceful enough to handle it properly. But he had to be careful with cab drivers. One travel guide gave this warning, even though hackney fares were fixed by law: "[T]hey are honest fellows…but they require close — very close — looking after…. They will charge you twice or thrice as much fare as the law allows."[14]

Nathaniel, Reed's brother, was in jail in Ravenna, Ohio, accused of breaking into a grocery store. Tending to his brother's predicament was the second objective of his trip.

The papers mailed home were probably newspapers. Penny papers were in great supply in New York City, and they provided inexpensive entertainment for all social classes. Cheap and widely distributed, the penny press departed from the traditional newspaper format that appealed primarily to upper- and middle-class readers. Published in the mornings and usually unaffiliated politically, penny papers focused on "local news, police reports, and city affairs."[15]

> *Gow and ingage passage to Phlidelpha. Pay for ticket $4.00. Inquire for the*

Merchants Hotell and find I am about 2 miles from it. Be gin to be in a hurray, fearful I shall loos Boat but got back in reason and went in to the Markett. It is curiosity to see what they have to sell. Could not help spending 25 cents.

Besides getting lost, Reed also had to cope with urban traffic congestion and the simple challenge of crossing a street: "To perform the feat with any degree of safety, you must button your coat tight about you, see that your shoes are secure at the heels, settle your hat firmly on your head, look up street and down street, at the self-same moment, to see what carts and carriages are upon you, and then run for your life."[16] All the while, watching your step as you avoided the mud and animal waste.

Reed was particularly impressed when visiting a market, but he did express some guilt about spending 25 cents. He would write in more detail the next day.

When Charles Dickens visited New York City in the spring of 1842, he had an experience much different from Reed's. He was taken by the "beautiful metropolis of America," but it was not as clean as Boston, where he had first set foot on these shores. Broadway was impressive, with shining pavement stones and many vehicles. The streets were filled with hackney cabs, carriages, coaches, and ladies with colorful parasols. Dickens lauded the "excellent hospitals and schools, literary institutions and libraries, an admirable fire department (as indeed it should be, having constant practice), and charities of every sort and kind."

But all was not so sublime. Pigs roamed freely in the streets. The "ugly brutes" were "city scavengers," not attended or fed, but left on their own. He visited the Five Points, where "[p]overty, wretchedness, and vice, are rife," safely escorted by two heads of police.

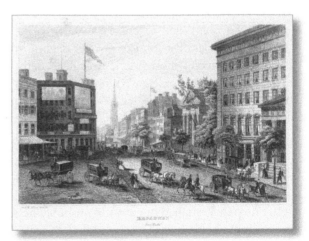

Broadway, c. 1840. Wikimedia Commons, public domain.

Welcomed by the upper classes, Dickens observed that "[t]he tone of the best society in this city, is like that of Boston; here and there, it may be, with a greater infusion of the mercantile spirit, but generally polished and refined, and always most hospitable. The houses and tables are elegant; the hours later and more rakish; and there is, perhaps, a greater spirit of contention in reference to appearances, and the display of wealth and costly living. The ladies are singularly beautiful."[17]

New York Cittey Sept 27 [25]—1841

Pay for lodgin 50 cents. Diner 50 cents. Cakes for supper 12½ cents.

2 oclock. Ben out vewing the shippin. It was agrand site to see them thick as they can be and from all parts of the wirld, Alodeing and on lodeing for miles. 3 oclock. Rains and blows verry hard, so that it was all most impossible to walk in the streets. The whitecaps on the water are aplenty. Looks pokerish, but I must gow on to Washington.

The Cab, New York City, by Nicolino Calyo (1799-1884),. http://bjws.blogspot.com/2012/11/life-in-streets-of-1840s-new-york-city.html.

Reed combined his business trip with some sightseeing. The tourist in him came out in several other spots: Washington, Pittsburgh, Akron, and Cleveland. Watching the comings and goings of the traffic on the water was a cherished spectator sport. The completion of the Erie Canal in 1825 had fortified New York City's role as the premier American port. Agricultural products were shipped from the interior of New York State, as well as Ohio and other western states, to the city, and manufactured goods were transported in the opposite direction. "One day in 1824 some 324 vessels were counted in New York harbor; on a day in 1836 there were 1,241."[18]

"View Of New York, From Brooklyn Heights," c. 1849. *New York Public Library Digital Collections, http://digitalcollections.nypl.org/items/510d47e0-d2fa-a3d9-e040-e00a18064a99* (accessed May 15, 2017).

Asa Greene, author of *A Glance at New York*, was also enthralled with watching the vessels on the water. But he recommended calmer weather and warmer temperatures. "It is perfectly delightful to take a station on the Battery, of a summer afternoon, and watch the vessels of all kinds, as they glide by, from the light skiff to the enormous steamboat, and from the fishing smack with a single sail, to the merchant ship with its thousand yards of canvas. It is charming to witness so busy a scene of life, and commerce, and pleasure, on the quiet bosom of the waves."[19]

Charles Dickens, too, enjoyed watching the antebellum water traffic. He approached New York City by sailing across Long Island Sound. He was met by "a forest of ships' masts, cheery with flapping sails and waving flags. Crossing among them to the opposite shore, were steam ferry-boats laden with people, coaches, horses, waggons, baskets, boxes: crossed and recrossed by other ferry-boats: all travelling to and fro: and never idle. Stately among these restless Insects, were two or three large ships, moving with slow majestic pace, as creatures of a prouder kind, disdainful of their puny journeys, and making for the broad sea."[20]

I jest ben in to the Markett. Cant think of any Provishion but what I can find hear. Frute of all kinds and a grate meney that I did not now [know] *the names of. Ded and live Poltry of different specas* [species]. *A grate meney differet from enney that I ever see before. Cattle, hogs, sheep, and dogs. One dog the smallist I ever see and as white as snow. Long shaggy hare. Prise $20.00 and was trimed in stile with red silk Ribin round his neck and bodey. Bought knife 50 cents.*

In the mid-1840s New York City had two major markets: Fulton (built in 1821) and Washington (1812). With Fulton near the East River and Washington near the Hudson River, both markets provided easy access to country suppliers of produce. Other smaller markets were distributed throughout the city. The goods available from the "victuallars" were meat, vegetables, fish, butter, and

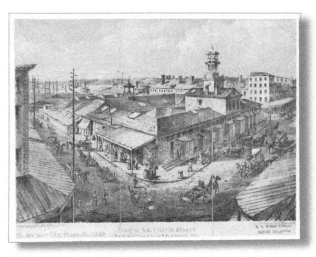

"Washington Market, N.Y.C., 1829." *New York Public Library Digital Collections, http://digitalcollections.nypl.org/items/510d47e0-d825-a3d9-e040-e00a18064a99* (accessed May 14, 2017).

cheese, among other things. The vast amount of business "will astonish the attentive observer," commented an antebellum guidebook, with the advice that "the morning is perhaps the most interesting time to visit."[21] With the city's location on the coast, the fish markets could offer a wide variety of seafood including oysters, shrimp, and lobster.

People went to the city market to socialize and view people of other classes. One mid-19th century observer pronounced that "'perhaps the chief attraction [of the Washington Market] lies in the essentially human character—in the bustle and the confusion, the rushing and the *tohu bohu* of the place. The rage which possesses both buyers and sellers, the concentration of purpose of so many thousands, the clangor of many voices, and the sounding of many footsteps, all impress themselves forcibly upon our imagination and appeal to our sympathies.'"[22]

The small dog Reed saw for sale for $20 was probably a Maltese, a toy dog covered with white silky fur. The breed has been documented for several thousand years as an "aristocrat" of the dog world.[23] The knife Reed purchased would have helped him eat the fruit he may have bought in the market.

> *I spent the most of the fore part of the day in seeing the colecttor to see if I could not git my patent with out gowing to Washington. But he told me to go to the Patent office. It would be the safest and most sure* [way] *to get a patent.*

Reed persisted in trying to secure his patent in New York City. If he had succeeded, he would have saved considerable time and money. But alas, he was convinced that proceeding to Washington was the best course.

● ● ● ● ● ● ● ● ●

*C*HAPTER 3
ON TO WASHINGTON

*O*nce again, Reed was on the move, this time on one of the country's first railroads.

[Saturday, September 25] *4 oclock for Phelidelpha. It has stop Raining and is verry Pleasant. It is a grand site to see the shippin as you leve the wharfe. Thare was 2 ships of war in cite as I left the wharfe to cros the River to Jersey. Took cares* [cars] *for Philidelpha. Past through a low wet country to Newark, thence to New Brunswick. A lowe redish soil of land, but the hay and grass looks verry well. The water along in the ditches looks verry red, all most as red as blood.*

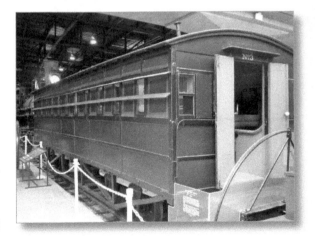

Reed could have been traveling in a rail car such as this Camden & Amboy Coach No. 3, now at the Railroad Museum of Pennsylvania. It had a seating capacity of 48 passengers. It is now the second oldest existing passenger rail car in America. Wikimedia Commons, public domain.

Reed traveled the Camden & Amboy rail line running south through New Jersey. It was the first railroad to operate in the state, completed in 1834, with a route from Camden to South Amboy. By 1840 it was "the first through all-rail line from New York to Philadelphia."[1] Reed's route from Philadelphia to Baltimore was on the Philadelphia, Wilmington & Baltimore Railroad; from Baltimore to Washington, he traveled on the Baltimore & Ohio line.[2]

The red soil Reed observed indicates the presence of iron oxide. Though the color is common from New Jersey southward, it was not something seen in Vermont.

New Brunswick is quite a lose place. Stop about one hour to wait for the other cares [cars]. *Bouht apease of pie, 2 aples, 8 cents.*

It is hard to determine what Reed meant by his description of New Brunswick as "lose." It could have been a comment about the perceived moral culture of this port town, as it provided "diversions" for the large number of working men of the growing transportation network. It was a stopping point for travelers between New York and Philadelphia and a grain shipping port for New Jersey. Two steamship lines serviced the town. The 1833 completion of the Delaware and Raritan Canal allowed coal and other freight to move more efficiently, and it provided a safer route between those big cities. The canal ran from Bordentown (below Trenton) on the Delaware River to New Brunswick on the Raritan River. Railroad connections soon followed. With this transportation network, New Brunswick became known as the "Hub City."[3]

Started and went about 2 houres and one of the care [car] *wheals broke and had to stop, but no one hirt. Hindered us about 1 hour. Had to take the care* [car] *off of the track and leave itt. Started agane and went though* [through] *a poor level sandy contry. The most the land is good for is to rase melons on.*

The technology of rail transport was in its infancy in the 1830s and 1840s, and these decades "yielded many casualties and small-scale accidents, but few major train wrecks."[4] The disregard for safety during this time was reflected in few double tracks, cost cutting in construction methods with sharp curves and steeper grades, unfenced tracks, crossings, and depots, and a minimum of state inspections and requirements. The era of telegraphs and dispatchers to keep track of trains had yet to arrive.[5]

Fortunately, the broken wheel on Reed's train did not lead to a more severe mishap. In the early years, cars rode the rails at a slow pace, no more than 18 miles per hour. Tracks were not built for high speed. There were not many trains running, and routes tended to be short. Night operation was very rare. A slow speed probably saved Reed's train from a worse fate. Passengers were killed in a few accidents, but such fatalities did not increase significantly until the 1850s.[6]

Rail travel had other drawbacks besides the threat of accidents. Its assault on the senses was onomatopoetically described by one 1840 adventurer: "[M]y sense of hearing was almost destroyed, by the continued fiz, fiz-fiz, fiz-fiz, fiz-fiz, of a steam engine, the incessant ding-ding, ding-ding, of the alarm bell, and the prolonged rumble, rumble, rumble of the rail car's wheels. My eyes, too, were well-nigh destroyed by sparks of fire, and flying ashes; but above all from the want of rest and sleep." The writer was elated to transfer to "an old-fashioned stage coach" in the Housatonic Valley of Connecticut.[7]

However, another 1840 traveler had an opposite experience during a trip from Boston to Portland, Maine. The first sixty miles to Portsmouth, New Hampshire, were covered in three hours in "rail cars, which for comfort, elegance, safety, and speed, are not to be surpassed, if equaled north, south, or west." From there, nine passengers were crowded into a mail stagecoach built for six. Two of them seated on the outside of the coach were soon inside, thoroughly drenched by the rain and possibly wishing for the luxurious accommodations of their previous rail coach.[8]

Charles Dickens was introduced to American railroads very early in his trip when he traveled from Boston to Lowell, Massachusetts, to tour the mills there. The cars were not delineated by first and second class, but rather by gender, so the men could smoke without women nearby. Men and women traveling together could ride in the women's car, as well as unescorted women who would "be certain of the most courteous and considerate treatment everywhere" across the country. There was a separate car for African Americans, "as a black man never travels with a white one." The cars, "like shabby omnibuses, but larger," held up to fifty passengers. Rows of seats set crosswise were separated by a "narrow passage" running along the middle. Each seat held two people, and a stove helped to heat the car. The ride was "jolting," noisy, and confined, with a minimum number of windows. Conversation between the passengers was constant, usually about politics, banks, and cotton.

The arrival in Lowell was marked by the engine "scattering in all directions a shower of burning sparks from its wood fire; screeching, hissing, yelling, panting; until at last the thirsty monster stops beneath a covered way to drink, the people cluster round, and you have time to breathe again."[9]

Arive at Philidelpha at 12 oclock at nite, but it is a verry pleasant Nite, all most as lite as day. Phelidelphia is averry hansom Cittey. Pay omnabuss driver at Phelidelphia for caring [carrying] *me through the Cittey to the Rail Road. (25 cents)*

Philadelphia was another big city for Reed; the 1840 population was 93,665, making it the fourth largest in nation. But he was just passing through.

The omnibus, a horse-drawn vehicle capable of carrying perhaps a dozen passengers, functioned as an urban version of the stagecoach. It ran a prescribed route, and it charged higher fares, limiting its clientele to the middle classes and above. The vehicles were designed to facilitate quick entry and exit by the passengers. When an omnibus approached a passenger's stop, a tug on a strap attached to the driver's ankle indicated the wish to get off. The omnibus originated

An omnibus, center, from a detail of "Panorama of Philadelphia. Chesnut Street, East of Fifth," c. 1856. Schnabel, Finkeldey & Demme, lithographer. Library of Congress.

in Europe and was on the streets of New York City by 1827. The 1830s were the heyday of their service in New York, with 108 in service by 1837. It was introduced in Philadelphia in 1831, running in the city center as well as some early suburbs. The omnibuses were eventually replaced by horse-drawn cars on rails that gave a smoother and faster ride.[10]

> *Phelidelphia Sept 28* [26] *1841*
>
> *Start 1 oclock in the morning for Baltimore. Paid for Tickett $4.00. Pass though a low wettish contry. Sunrise Sunday morning, Sept 28* [26], *verry pleasant, but rather cold. See some corne fields, but verry poor. It is planted 4 feet apart one way and 3 the other. Onley one stalk to the hill and I could not see but one ear to the stalk. The top of the stoks was cut off and all of the leafs were taken off of the stalk and that left the naked stalk standing looking like a fieled of bean pooles* [poles] *set jest after you had planted the beens. Some of the ears were as much as 5 feet from the ground.*

Why was Reed so interested in what he saw in the cornfields? Probably because it was most likely a departure from what he was used to in Vermont. Dr. Robert L. Nielsen, extension corn specialist and professor of agronomy at Purdue University, offered this explanation:

> [T]here were three primary strategies for hand harvest of corn in the mid-1800s. One was to cut the stalks, stack them in shocks and allow the ear corn to further dry, and eventually feed the crop in its entirety to their livestock. The

second was to cut the tops and remove the leaves for livestock fodder but leave the "naked" stalks standing with the ears still attached (as the journal describes) for later harvest of the ears. The third was to harvest and husk the ears from the standing stalks as is, and later cut the remainder of the stover for use as animal fodder or simply allow the animals to feed on the stover in the field.[11]

> *Arive at Baltimore at 8 oclock, Sunday morning Sept 28 [26]. At Baltimore thay are not allowed to gow in the cittey with the steam cares [cars]. And thay left the steam car and hitch on 4 of nisest looking horses I ever see and went about a mile and in turning a corner run off the track and run aganst a building. No damage excepting the braking of the tung. Got out of care [car] and walked 1½ miles to the Washington Rail Road Depoint [depot]. Thare I see 20 or 25 of the best horses I ever see.*

Once again Reed's luck held in the face of a rail accident. The "tung" was the pole on the front of the car where the horses were attached with the harnesses.

New York City had banned steam engines in lower Manhattan after an 1834 explosion.[12] With the ever-increasing demand for space on its city streets between wagons, carriages, omnibuses, walkers, and rail lines, Philadelphia responded by outlawing steam engines in 1838. This ban pushed depots beyond the established urban boundaries.[13]

Reed was correct about a steam engine ban in Baltimore. In addition to the safety concern and need to reduce traffic on the streets, when a city was served by different rail lines, such as Baltimore in 1841, there was usually a depot for each line, often in separate parts of the city, necessitating travel between depots to continue a journey. Later in the 1800s "union stations" were built in the cities to combine the comings and goings of various rail lines. This simplified travel and eliminated awkward and time-consuming transfers for passengers.[14]

> *Gow to the Rail road office to git tickett for Washington, but am told that my money is not worth eny thing, that the Bank has broke. What to do now? I [k]now not. 4 hundred miles from home and only one dollar in eny money, exceptting Burlington Bank bills. Gow to another office. Try to git some changed, cant. Gow to another off[ice], 25 br [per] cent discount. Thay say it is not wirth 12 cents on the dollar in passing. A man offores [offers] to change it with me and give me Rail road money. Change 4 dollars with him and git my tickett and take my seat for Washington. Pay for tickett $2.50.*

Reed was feeling the effects of the Panic of 1837, an economic depression that continued well into the 1840s. Railroad and canal construction dropped off severely, prices and wages declined, unemployment increased, and land values decreased.

The charter of the Second Bank of the United States had expired in 1836, and given the unpopularity of a powerful central bank, it was not renewed. The country entered a period of erratic "free banking," where state-chartered banks, railroads, insurance companies, and manufacturing concerns could issue their own paper money and regulations were minimal. The value of any currency held by an individual was dependent upon the stability of the issuing institution. Reed solved his immediate problem but paid a price.[15]

Charles Dickens called the United State Bank "the Tomb of many fortunes… The stoppage of this bank, with its ruinous consequences, had cast (as I was told on every side) a gloom on Philadelphia, under the depressing effect of which, it yet laboured."[16]

> *Rather down harted, but hoping for better times. Pas along though a little better contry. See aplenty of Nigrows and som tobaco plantations. The land is what I should call poor. It is corse gravel soil, not but very few cattle.*

Here is one of the few times that Reed expressed any emotion in a journal entry. Evidently, the challenge to his money in the Baltimore rail depot had him worried about his ability to continue the trip, secure a patent, and head to Ohio to help his brother Nathaniel. In the margin, he tabulated the money spent up to this point. His expenses from Essex, Vermont, to Washington, D.C., came to $24.65. He subtracted $3.65 as "imnessary" [unnecessary] and noted a total $21.00. Reed's frugal nature appeared again in his accounting of expenses. It is possible that the journey was financed, at least in part, by his father or other family members. If so, Reed had one more reason to be careful with his money.

Given the small number of African Americans in Vermont, it is not surprising that Reed would comment on seeing them working in the fields. Just the sight of them was novel for this resident of a very white state. In the 1840 census, the largest number of African Americans in any one Vermont town was 67 in Rutland, or 2.5 percent of the town's population. Of the top six communities with the largest number of black residents, no town had a higher percentage than Rutland. Two towns in Reed's Chittenden County, Burlington and Hinesburgh, were listed in the top six, so it was possible he had some experience in relating to African Americans prior to his trip south.[17]

Charles Dickens stopped in Baltimore for a meal served by slaves. This was one issue he did not hold back on. "The sensation of exacting any service from human creatures who are bought and sold, and being, for the time, a party as it were to their condition, is not an enviable one. The institution exists, perhaps, in its least repulsive and most mitigated form in such a town as this; but it is slavery; and though I was, with respect to it, an innocent man, its presence filled me with a sense of shame and self-reproach."[18]

Social critic and author Frances Trollope's distaste for slavery, and Americans' unjust treatment of the Indians, also brought a strong condemnation. The hypocrisy of America's "eternal boast of liberality and the love of freedom" was displayed when they were "with one hand hoisting the cap of liberty, and with the other flogging their slaves."[19]

Although he didn't comment about slavery, Reed made additional observations about the African Americans he saw in Washington, his next stop.

· · · · · · · ·

*C*HAPTER 4
WASHINGTON, D.C.

eed reached Washington and immediately his luck with his accommodations changed, much to his delight.

[Sunday, September 26 continued] *Arive at Washington at 11 oclock
near the capital. Aplenty of carages to carry pasengers, but I take my valese in
my hand and walk Down the st*[reet]. *Stop at the firs bublick* [public] *hous,
not nowing whether I can pay for a nite lodgein or not.*

Sunday, Sept. 29 [26]. *Take my seat in the setting room, for thare was no bare
[bar] room, it being a temberance house cep by Isaac Beers. And I think it one
of the bes houses I ben in senc I left home.*

On this part of his journey, Reed was traveling light, certainly an advantage
given the variety of the modes of transport he was using. Later, as he was leaving Cleveland and headed home, he had more luggage. The value of his money
brought about the worry of affording a room.

Isaac Beers' hotel was listed as a temperance house in the local newspaper. It
was located on Pennsylvania Avenue near 4½ Street and was such a landmark that
several businesses, such as a periodical agency and a book bindery, advertised that
they were located nearby.

A local newspaper complimented Mr. Beers, as it editorialized about the hypocrisy of temperance leaders who patronized establishments that sold ardent spirits.
"Why is this so? Is it because they like secret indulgence, or for want of moral

courage to identify themselves with temperance houses? In this city we have only one Temperance house, not surpassed by any, (kept by Mr. Isaac Beers), at a point 'where people do congregate' from every portion of the United States, and yet how poorly the worthy proprietor has been sustained."[1] Reed's mood must have picked up with his good fortune in finding a reputable temperance house.

> *It being Sunday I think it is aplay day for the Black people. And it is sport to sit and vew them pasing and strutting with segars in thare mouths and appearing as happy as eny people I ever see. Som of them are dres as nise as eny peopple I ever see and some as poor.*

BLACK AND WHITE BEAUX.

Francis Trollope was very much taken by this African American couple as they strolled about "in the extreme of fashion" one Sunday in New York City. The man exhibited "tender devotion" to his "sable goddess." In contrast, in the window "stood a very pretty white girl, with two gentlemen beside her; but alas! both of them had their hats on, and one was smoking!" "Black and White Beaux," *Domestic Manners of the Americans*, 279.

Washington was a southern city where slavery flourished; the auction sites and pens, as well as the sight of coffles, or lines of slaves chained together, marching through the streets, were daily reminders that the promise of equality for all had a long way to go. The population of Washington, D.C., in 1840 was 43,711. Of this total, 30,657 were white and 13,054, or about 30 percent, were African American (8,360 free, and 4,694 slaves.)[2] One historian called it a "bifurcated city."[3]

Reed must have observed African American people in New York City, where over 16,000 lived in 1840, still a very small percentage of the total population of approximately 312,710.[4]

Nevertheless, he was probably unused to seeing so many African American people in public. His stereotype of how they should dress and behave was challenged. Was he expecting just misery and poverty? Was it possible that some of them had enough income to dress well? Sunday was a traditional day off for slaves. Some of the "strutting" people were probably free African Americans who would have had access to wardrobes of a finer cut.

Reed was probably aware of one incident that illustrated the tensions between the races: the *Amistad* case. In violation of existing treaties, in February 1839 Portuguese slave traders seized Africans from Sierra Leone and put them on a transport to Cuba, where they were to be sold. The Africans took over the ship, killed the captain and one other crew member, and demanded to be taken back to Africa. The ship was seized by the United States government brig *Washington*, and the Africans ended up in jail in New Haven, Connecticut. In January 1841 the case came before the Supreme Court, where former president John Quincy Adams successfully argued for the Africans' freedom. The Court agreed and thirty-five of them returned to their home.

> *2 oclok, eat dinner 3 oclock. Start to vew the capital. It is sittuated on a rise of ground, something like the cologe [college] at Burlington, [Vermont]. I walked to the upper part of the bilding and entered a yard containing about 2 acres with shade trees and flowers set in the handsomes maner thay can be. In the center is a Fish Pond about 35 feet long and 25 wide in the shape of an egg. The sides of it are hewd ston and thare is constantly a stream of water Runing in. And thare is quite a number of fish, and the water pases under the house, and runs out in to ston wash bole that will hold about 4 pailes full, Whare thay gow to drink and wash from. Thence to an other bond [pond] in the center which is a monument erected to the memory of som of our galant contry men. From thence to another bond [pond] about 200 feet lower down which is constructed that it raines all of the time; it runs in to the pond. It is done by the means of pipes with strainer on the end which the water ceeps in a constant whirl as it runs in. And it spirts up about 10 or 12 feet in the senter and that causes a rain bo[w] when the sun shines and is quite a curiosity. The lower yard is rather larger than the upper one and is shaded by a grate meney trees and both yards are fenced with iron fencs and two men to gard the bilding. On the front side of the house is 20 or 25 steps to git up to the level of the upper yard. It is verry pleasant to stand on the steps and look out to the Cittey.*

Reed described the west side of the Capitol. The Tripoli Monument, "erected to the memory of som of our galant contry men," honored six naval officers who died in the First Barbary War (1801-1805). Though Reed was impressed by the monument's location, one admiral disapproved. "And to cap the climax of absurdity, the Naval Monument had, as an evil omen I presume, been placed in a small circular pond of dirty fresh water—not large enough for a duck puddle—to represent the Mediterranean Sea."[5]

In 1841 the U.S. Capitol looked quite different than it does today. It was considerably smaller, for several wings and extensions have been added, and the original dome has been replaced.

Reed continued to tour the city.

The Presidents house is sittuated rite in frunt of the capital about one mile from it. The Presidents house is a nise building, but not so nise as I expected from what I had herd about it. I['ve] ben and vew the new Patent office. It is one of the Nices bildings in the states, of hewn ston about 200 feet long, 3 stores high. It will cost as much as 200 [t]housand dollars. Thence to the New Post office. It is of hewn ston, verry large and the most wirk man ship I ever see on anny building. The window caseing is of ston and the Jet [projection] is wirk out of ston, verry Nise. I ben most over the Cittey. It is pleasantly situated, but not as large as I expectted. 8 oclock went to bed, slept well.

Reed's favorite building, the Patent Office, was barely finished when he visited in 1841. The grand, three-story building with a columned entry portico dominated its square just a few blocks north of Pennsylvania Avenue at the intersection of two busy streets. Construction on it had started in 1836, but a disastrous fire later that year destroyed all the existing patent records and models submitted up to that time and stored in a former hotel. A design for the building by William Parker Elliot (1807-1854) was chosen by a Senate committee, but President Andrew Jackson also appointed Robert Mills, a more experienced architect, to oversee the project, and it is his work that gives the building distinction. Reed saw the first, southern part of a four-part structure eventually built around an open courtyard. The building now serves as the Smithsonian American Art Museum and the National Portrait Gallery.[6]

The west side of the Capitol in 1831, by John Rubens Smith. The Tripoli Monument is visible in the center. Library of Congress.

The neoclassical Post Office building, designed by Robert Mills and across the street to the southeast from the Patent Office, was built between 1839 and 1842, then enlarged in the 1850s and 1860s. Two U-shaped structures enclose a courtyard. What Reed referred to as "hewn ston" is marble, sandstone, and granite.[7] The Post Office building is now the Kimpton Hotel Monaco.

The President's House, south side, in 1846. It became officially known as the White House in 1901 under President Theodore Roosevelt. Library of Congress.

"United States Patent Office, Washington, D.C., showing F Street facade, possibly taken from the upper floor of the General Post Office," c. 1846. Library of Congress.

"General Post Office from the corner of 8th Street and E Street, NW, Washington, D.C., the shop of Elija Dyer, merchant tailor, on the left," c. 1846. Library of Congress.

Monday, September 30, [27] 1841

Pleasant but cold. Ben to the Brokers and can git silver for one cent discount on the money I have got. Went to the Patent office. Found I could not do enny thing with out drafts and other papers. Went to Doct Jones. He would not make them without 25 dollars for his fee. Went to E. P. Elleot. His clirk offored to do it for 15 dollars. Went to breckfast, got shaved and hare cut. 37½ cents. Catch 3 fishes. Went back to Patent office, vewed the moddles. Found none like mine.

Reed has changed his bank bills into silver at a broker, paying a one-cent fee on the exchange. When he arrived at the Patent Office he found that he must adhere to strict regulations to obtain a patent. He needed a technical drawing of his carriage springs invention, and he had to pay a fee. The Patent Office also required each inventor to submit a working model of the invention, along with the documentation. The models had to conform to a space of a cubic foot. This would help establish the uniqueness of the invention, as it was placed against those of a similar nature. He probably had arrived with a model of his invention in hand, so when he surveyed the others, he was relieved to find that none resembled his. This would make receiving a patent somewhat easier. It was not as if he was without competition. Seven other patents for various carriage springs were approved from 1839 to 1841.[8]

Dr. Thomas Jones, M.D. ("Doct Jones"), was appointed superintendent of the Patent Office by Secretary of State Henry Clay on April 12, 1828. His tenure was marked with controversy and he served only until June 10, 1829. Apparently, though, Jones was still available to do technical drawings for applicants at the time of Reed's visit. "E. P. Elleot" may have been a reference to William Parker Elliot, the man who submitted drawings for the design of the Patent Office building, and, at the time of Reed's visit, was a proprietor of a nearby patent agency.

Frances Trollope visited the Patent Office before the 1836 fire and characterized it "as a curious record of the fertility of the mind of man when left to its own resources; but it gives ample proof also that it is not under such circumstances [that] it is most usefully employed."[9]

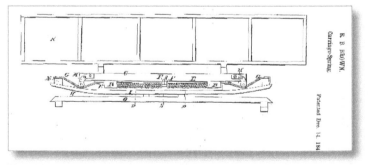

The side view of a wagon body with springs attached from Reed's patent drawing. "To all whom it may concern Be it known that I, R. B. BROWN, of Essex, in the county of Chittenden and State of Vermont, have invented a new and useful Improvement in Springs for Carriages, Wagons, &c." United States Patent Office.

In 1841, there were 847 patent applications; 58 percent, or 490, were granted. Reed's application for his carriage springs was approved on December 14, 1841, and given the patent number of 2385. Evaluating the invention, two present-day experts thought it excessively complex. Paul Wood, a Vermont historian and authority on 19th-century inventions, opined that, "the practical success of this design probably depends on the flexibility, strength and durability of the bands or straps."[10] Randy Kirschner of Fort Saint John, British Columbia, Canada, a wheel-wright and restorer of wagons and carriages, wrote that, "It seems over complicated for what it does. More likely to have maintenance problems than leaf springs. Too many parts."[11]

Wood explained Reed's knack for inventiveness this way:

I believe the inventiveness of blacksmiths comes from the material itself — iron. A skilled blacksmith can form iron into an almost endless variety of shapes which are both strong and long-lasting. For this reason, farmers, craftsmen, and others came to the blacksmith for repairs and to design and build new solutions to their problems. As the 19th century progressed, iron became cheaper and more available and so made up an ever-larger part of the materials employed. Not all blacksmiths were inventive, but those who were, saw the possibilities of solving new problems with iron. Blacksmiths had to be problem solvers, usually the more difficult problems, since farmers and craftsmen could solve the simple problems themselves. So problem-solving skills, plus the ability to craft versatile iron into tentative solutions made the blacksmith a natural inventor.[12]

Like other inventors, Reed's innovation came out of his mechanical aptitude encouraged when he undoubtedly apprenticed with his father, also a blacksmith. Reed was involved in a patent-granting process, authorized by the Constitution, that had become symbolic of and essential to the increasing growth of American technology. Transportation, manufacturing, and farming were undergoing revolu-tionary changes in the hands of these practical creators, and the recently improved patent procedure was of great benefit to the applicants. The process led to the "de-mocratization of invention" whereby an ordinary citizen, like Reed Brown, could, with a modest fee, take advantage of the professional staff at the patent office and expect a fair and impartial review of his application. Unlike France and Britain, the United States did not limit patents to affluent elites. An applicant could contest a patent office ruling through the judiciary, all the way to the Supreme Court. The patent process was transparent, and the resulting granted patents were published on a regular basis. The Patent Office became a centralized source of information on the growth of American technology. This egalitarian approach made the office very busy, as the number of applications and patents granted during the antebellum period increased significantly.[13]

Washington, D. C. Sept 30—1841 [September 27]

Went to the clirk for advise whether to git Dr. Jones or Elliot to transact the business. Advised me to git Mr. Ellott. Went and ingaged him to make the nesessary papers and paid him his fee $15. Went and got the silver to pay for Patent, paid discount, 30 cents. Paid in to the office for Patent, $30.

I then went to vewing the different models. It was a grand site to see them. Wirth 6 cents to 2 thousand dollars. Abeas [And best] *of all kinds you can think of, from a gimbleitt to a Steam boat.*

A "gimbleitt" (gimlet) was defined by Webster's 1828 Dictionary as "a borer; small instrument with a pointed screw at the end, for boring holes in wood by turning. It is applied only to small instruments; a large instrument of the like kind is called an auger."[14]

The Patent Office building had more surprises in store for Reed.

After vewing the moddles till I was tired of it, I went in to the upper room, whare thare is the Publick Museum. I thare see the dress that Gen. Washington had on when he recived his comishion. It Was a blew coat faced with a puff [buff] *collar, verry corse buttons, as large as a 50 ct pease. Buff collar vest and britches. All what would be coled verry cors now. Thare is a gold snuff box with Pearles set in the lid that was given of the Preident of som foren poure* [some foreign power] *valued $35. A Pearl Neclace given to Vanburen $35. A gold scabered sword with dimonds in the hilt $3,000.*

Thare shahols [shawls] *that have be presented to the Ladys of the Presidents, wirth from 5 to 12 hundred dollars. The horse blanketts that was on the horse sent to M. Vanburan that ware* [were] *sold at Auction, verry Nise. The seal of the U.S.A. is a hansom thing. It is about 4 inches acrost it, and there is two cords that look as if they were made of gold, and a large tastle on each, and the cord has to pas though under the ceal. Thare is the profiles of Most of the Indian warrers painted in thare ware* [war] *dress and some of them that will all most make a man shudder to look at them. Thare is Indian wirk of all most everry kind, even to a bark canoo, day harnises, Ware* [war] *clubs, and the dresses of the differnt tribes. Mummez from New Zeland and other contryes, som in a sitting poster* [posture]. *Birds stufed of all speces: one black and white crow, one shark. And finely, to meney things to menshon. The declaration of the Independence, the firs one that was sined.*

Reed had happened upon the precursor of the Smithsonian Institution. The collection of gifts from foreign leaders, biological specimens, United States historical objects, and other curiosities came from a variety of places. The most amazing source, the Wilkes Expedition, or more properly, the United States Exploring Expedition, was carried out by the Navy over four years (1838-1842). The goal was to expand scientific knowledge, establish diplomatic ties around the Pacific Ocean, produce more detailed charts for American ships, and add knowledge about the Pacific Northwest coast. The expedition consisted of "six sailing vessels and 346 men, including a team of nine scientists and artists, making it one of the largest voyages of discovery in the history of Western exploration." They sailed around South America, visited islands in the South Pacific, Australia, Antarctica, New Zealand, Fiji, and the west coast of South and North America, and returned to the east coast of the United States via the Philippines, around South Africa, and across the Atlantic to New York City, where they landed on June 10, 1842.[15] They collected artifacts from other cultures, as well as plant and animal specimens. The estimated total of 40 tons of amassed material eventually made its way back to the United States, often transferred to American ships returning to the US that the expedition met on their voyages. On February 8, 1841, 150 boxes of material from the expedition were shipped from Philadelphia to Washington, D.C. The boxes were headed to the Patent Office building, for as early as 1836 this was slated as the central depository for "a national museum of the arts." In April 1841, the dampness of the storage in the basement of the building prompted the items to be moved to the grand hall on the third floor.

An 1841 patent model for a machine that automated the process of manufacturing pins. Models were required to be no larger than a cubic foot. Invented by John I. Howe, patent number 2013. This is the type of model Reed would have seen in the Patent Office Museum. Photograph by the author.

Joining the artifacts and specimens from the Exploring Expedition at the Patent Office were Native American portraits and "curiosities" from the War Department, and gems and minerals from James Smithson's collection. Smithson was an English scientist who left a considerable sum of money to the United States "to found at Washington, under the name of the Smithsonian Institution, an Establishment for the increase & diffusion of knowledge among men." The items from the Exploring Expedition were later transferred to the Smithsonian and contributed to its widely admired reputation as a leader in scientific research.[16]

Three documents help shed some detailed light on the museum pieces in the Patent Office that Reed described in his journal. On June 11, 1841, Secretary of State Daniel Webster wrote a letter to Commissioner of Patents Henry L. Ellsworth containing an inventory of artifacts that were soon to be transferred to the Patent Office. Since many of the items were gifts from foreign leaders, it was natural that they were kept under the secretary of state's office. Webster had learned that the Patent Office had "suitable accommodations for the safe-keeping, as well as the exhibition of the various articles." Thus, Ellsworth was instructed to keep them "convenient and secure," and available for public viewing. The inventory includes some detail on the origin of some of the items.[17]

The second source is *A Popular Catalogue of the Extraordinary Curiosities in the National Institute Arranged in the Building Belonging to the Patent Office*, published by Alfred Hunter in 1855.[18.] The third document is De Benneville Randolph Keim's 1874 *Illustrated Guide to the Museum of Models, Patent Office*. Keim included some detail about the artifacts that were still in the Patent Office museum at this later date.[19]

Webster's 1841 letter reveals that "a gold snuff box, set with diamonds, [was a] present to Levitt Harris, when Charge d'Affaires at St. Petersburg."

The sword Reed valued at $3,000 was in Keim's guide: "A sword, originally with diamond studded hilt and gold scabbard, presented by the Spanish Viceroy of Peru to Commodore James Biddle, U.S.N., while cruising of the Pacific coast about 1830."[20]

After viewing these various gifts from foreign leaders, and learning about a law requiring the objects to be kept by the government to "prevent the possibility of bribery" of our envoys, Frances Trollope offered her view: "I should think it would be a better way to select for the office such men as they felt could not be seduced by a sword or a snuff-box. But they, doubtless, know their own business best."[21]

The shawls mentioned by

Reed viewed the patent models and assorted curiosities in this section of what is now the National Portrait Gallery and American Art Museum of the Smithsonian Institution. Photograph by the author.

Reed were explained in Alfred Hunter's guide. "Under the shelf are six valuable Cashmere shawls, of the value of $1,200, presents from the Imaum [Imam] of Muscat; one presented to the wife of Lieut. W. F. Shields, the commander of the U.S. Schooner *Boxer*, a striped one to the wife of Lieut. A. W. Foote, the rest to Martin Van Buren, the president. According to law, they were obliged to be deposited here."[22].

The seal of the United States is mentioned in Hunter's guide, but since additional details are not provided, we must depend on Reed's description.[23]

The paintings of the Indian warriors that would make a man "shudder" were noted by Hunter. "The visitor will have observed along the wall numerous portraits of Indians, but the most noted ones are only named, and they are placed too high up to discern the feature closely. They were painted by order of the War Department."[24]

Hunter mentions a wide variety of Indian artifacts from various parts of the country. He also cites mummies from Peru and Egypt, but none from New Zealand. But he did go into a lengthy description of tattooed heads and how they became illegal as trading items between Australia and New Zealand.[25]

Yes, the original Declaration of Independence was there, mentioned in the Daniel Webster letter. Reed had happened upon the premier museum in the nation's capital, apparently without a prior plan. He had slipped into a tourist role and obviously enjoyed it a great deal.

> *12 o'clock. Ben to see if my* [patent] *Papers are redey. Can't git them till 4 oclock. Went to dinner and then to see the President, but he was not at home. Vewed the house And it is nott as nise as I expectted. Thare is a verry nise yard around it which is shaded and laid out in the handsomes maner.*

Reed hoped to see President John Tyler (1790-1862), who had been elected vice president in 1840 on the Whig ticket but assumed the higher office when President William Henry Harrison died on April 4, 1841, just 32 days into his term. When Tyler set his own path by not following the dictates of the Whig Party, he was expelled from the party and his popularity plummeted, but he served out the term, to 1845.

It was just a matter of bad timing that Reed was not able to meet with President Tyler. Charles Dickens did visit the "President's mansion" twice during his 1842 Washington stay. Of the grounds, he wrote, "The ornamental ground about it has been laid out in garden walks; they are pretty, and agreeable to the eye; though they have that uncomfortable air of having been made yesterday, which is far from favourable to the display of such beauties."[26]

As for President Tyler, Dickens allowed that he was rather unpopular and "looked somewhat worn and anxious, and well he might: being at war with everybody—but the expression on his face was mild and pleasant, and his manner was remarkably unaffected, gentlemanly, and agreeable. I thought that in his whole carriage and demeanour, he became his station singularly well."[27]

President John Tyler. Library of Congress.

Reed's wish to visit the president now seems strange, given the current tight security around all government buildings in Washington. But for most of the 19th century the president's house and grounds were generally open to the public. "[T]he iron gates to the White House grounds opened at 8 in the morning and closed at sundown. Almost anyone was likely to wander [the well-manicured gardens], along the paths," states White House historian William Seale.[28]

To actually meet with the president, "you could come into the White House without security checks, up to the second floor where the president's offices were…, sit in the waiting room and if you are willing to wait, you might get lucky and get an interview with the president or ask him a question or two," according to historian Dr. William B. Bushong.[29]

> *From thence to the capitol. Went in and vewed the rooms whare we pay men 8 dollars a day for abuse to one another. In one Room, thare is the Paintings of all the old Publick officers as large as life, The Paintings of Indians. Thare is a grate meney ston Images, sutch as the Wm. Pens. treaty, Pohontas saveing Capt. Smith, and others that I did not now. Thes ston images are as large as life and look verry nise. Thay are up in the sides of the wall--the part in side of the building. Look as if thay were made of small stons sutch as you can find in the banks of Rivers. The post are round and as smooth as glass.*
>
> *5 oclock sundown and supper redeay. Spent in corse of the day: two apples 4 cents, oath on petishion 25 cents, pencils points 12½ cents, two books 20 cents.*

The comment about "abuse" reflects Reed's low opinion of the nature of debate in Congress. These deliberations revealed differing viewpoints on many topics and disagreements were often extreme. Slavery was the dominant issue of the day and provided the underlying tension evident among the members of Congress.

Reed was in the rotunda of the Capitol, a circular room now 96 feet in diameter and 180 feet in height. The building was started in 1793 when George Washington laid the cornerstone. The original building was completed in 1826, following rebuilding after it was burned by the British during the War of 1812. The Capitol has undergone numerous changes, additions, and renovations through the years to arrive at what we now know as the seat of our national government.

The four "ston images" Reed observed were carved into the sandstone walls in relief as part of the restoration of the Capitol after the fire of 1814. He recognized the William Penn and the Pocahontas carvings. The other two scenes he was not familiar with were *Conflict of Daniel Boone and the Indians, 1773*, and *Landing of the Pilgrims, 1620*. Surely, he must have learned about the Pilgrims at Plymouth Rock, an often-recounted story in 19th-century common schools.

"Preservation of Captain Smith by Pocahontas, 1606." Antonio Capellano, artist, sandstone, 1825, located in the Capitol rotunda, above the west door. Architect of the Capitol website.

Under his expenses, Reed noted an "oath on petishion," possibly part of the patent application process. The "pencil points" are probably a reference to his use of pencils for the initial writing in a smaller diary or notebook while on the road.

This morning it was verry cold so that I shock [shook] with the cold. At noon it was verry warm.

Washington, D. C. Sept 30 [27]—1841

The land at Washington and vercinity is verry Poor of a corse gravelly soil. I did not see as much to live on growing in the Cittey as I raised in my garding [garden]. Thare is acres of land laying abou to the comons that would starve a grass hopper.

The farmer in Reed led him to pass judgment on the poor soil and wasted common land of the city. Although he was impressed with the grand architecture, he would not miss the "ramshackle, chaotic, dirty, and dangerously insalubrious town . . . foreign visitors who arrived to see American democracy at work (or be confirmed in their lofty ironies about it) almost always commented on the disparity between reality and the grandeur of the original design."[30]

Charles Dickens had this final thought on Washington, D.C. "It is sometimes called the City of Magnificent Distances, but it might with greater propriety be termed the City of Magnificent Intentions; for it is only on taking a bird's-eye view of it from the top of the Capitol that one can at all comprehend the vast designs of its projector, an aspiring Frenchman [Pierre Charles L'Enfant]. Spacious avenues that begin in nothing, and lead nowhere; streets, mile-long, that only want houses, roads, and inhabitants; public buildings that need but a public to be complete; and ornaments of great thoroughfares, which only lack great thoroughfares to orna- ment -- are its leading features."[31]

Reed's business transactions were done in Washington; he was now on a mis- sion to connect with his brother who was in jail in Ohio. He was about to embark on the most trying leg of his journey.

. . . .

CHAPTER 5

ACROSS PENNSYLVANIA

fter several days in Washington, D.C., Reed could leave town knowing his patent application was taken care of, and with a greater appreciation of the nature of the nation's capital.

Tusday Morning Oct 1st [September 28] *1842* [1841]. *Git up, eat breck-fes, and settle with the land lord and pay him for 3 days borde, $2.75. Verry pleasant and start for home. Pay for tickett to Baltimore, $2.50. Stop 9 miles short at the Leway house, and wait for cares* [cars] *to Frederick, Pensylvania, fare $2.50. Git ticket at Leway to Brownsvill, $12.00.*

Reed was not headed home; he was about to travel across southern Pennsylvania in a stagecoach on his way to Ohio. He journeyed through the night and missed recording the names of some of the towns and stops, and his exact route is not clear from his journal entries. He was overcome with exhaustion, so there is a good chance his sketchy record of this section of his trip was recorded after he arrived in Pittsburgh. Depending on road conditions, stagecoach travel could be notoriously rough and bumpy, and certainly not conducive to journal writing. His weariness also added to the challenge of remembering and recording his exact route. When he started in Maryland, he was definite on what the route was. But for some reason, he turns Relay House into "Leway House" and he places Frederick in Pennsylvania, not Maryland.

The first rail cars on the Baltimore & Ohio line were drawn by horses 13 miles between Mount Claire Station in Baltimore and Ellicott's Mills. This location to make the change, or relay, of horses became known as Relay House ("Leway house"). The original 32-room structure on this site served as a train depot, tavern, and hotel. With the replacement of horse-drawn cars by steam engines by 1836, Relay House had become a water stop for the engines and an important transfer point for travelers like Reed.[1]

Reed's probable route was from Relay House, and then by rail to Frederick, Maryland. From there he went through Littlestown, Pennsylvania, then probably to Gettysburg to take the Pittsburgh Pike. He traveled to Brownsville and eventually Pittsburgh.[2]

> *Pas though a poor contry, few tobaco plantations and Nigrows a plenty. I have not seen enny thing growing to live on, excepting corn, and that verry poor. No wonder that the hogs can run in the cornfields. For the best hog that I have seen in 4 or 5 dayes would not weigh 50 lbs, and the worst I have seen are a curious sort, for thare bristles stand pinted towards thare heads.*

One expert on heritage animals stated that, "This is unlikely to have been a reference to a specific hog breed…. [but] might have been a local population with a single-gene change something like Rhodesian Ridgebacks. Alternatively, these might have been pigs so stunted by malnutrition that their hair coats became abnormal."[3]

Frederick PA [Maryland] *Oct 1ˢᵗ* [September 28] *1842* [1841]. *I have seen 15 or 20 sheep. The firs I have seen in this contry are of the old Native kind. Thare is but a few cattle to be seen. A few horses, but in general verry poor. 9 oclock start from Leway house for Frederick, and the contry grows better. Pas up a River and some good land, timber, mostley oak, rather mountainous and agrate meney Mills.*

The Relay House in 1857. An engraving in *Harper's Monthly Magazine*, "June Jaunt," 14 (April 1857): 592-612.

Meet a grate meney Pensylvania teams, but the horses are small and poor. But the Wagons and harneses are large enough to make it. Arive at Frederick at 12 oclock. Diner, 37½ cents.

Reed had his first look at the Conestoga wagons with "Pensylvania teams" that served as freight haulers on the turnpikes. The history of these wagons goes back to the mid-18th century section of the state around the town of Conestoga in Lancaster County. The design of the wagon was unique, with the ends higher than the middle to reduce the shifting of cargo, large wide wheels to handle uneven road conditions, and hickory hoops covered with white canvas drawn tight to protect the contents.

The freight wagons were built for heavy-duty work in mountainous areas. They could be 18 feet long and 21 feet tall and could handle up to five tons pulled by six strong horses, although 6,000 pounds was more typical. The most common load was grain. One early 20th-century regional history stated that the "Great Conestoga wagons [were] laden with merchandise, flour, whisky, bacon and other products on their eastward trip and iron, salt and other merchandise on their westward trip."[4]

With no seats, the wagoner had three options: walk alongside the wagon, ride one of the horses, or pull out what was called a lazy board and take a break on a rough seat.

The wagoners drove in groups of six to eight to help each other in case of trouble and breakdowns, as they shared the roads with livestock such as horses, cattle, sheep, hogs, driven from the west to eastern cities.[5]

A model of a Conestoga wagon. This heavy, rugged wagon was not the same as the lighter covered wagon made famous later by settlers migrating west. *Popular Science Monthly*, Volume 58.

A verry pleasant and hansom plase [Frederick, Maryland], *about as large as Burlington. Thare was 7 stages awaiting, start for Pittsburgh. Pass some nise farmes whare thay have from 25 to 100 acres of wheat in a field. It is quite curious to see the Dutch men aploughing with 3 horse on a plough with onley 1 line. Thay plough left handed. To Littleton 13 miles. The land in general layes in swells about ¾ of a mile from one ridge to another. The land is verry good but rather Mountainous and verry poorley watered.*

Assuming Reed was traveling in a Concord coach, he was in one of the 1,800 coaches that were built between 1827 and 1899 by the Abbott-Downing Company of Concord, New Hampshire. Carrying six, nine, or twelve passengers, they were pulled by two, four, or six horses. The round body of the coach was suspended on leather strips called throughbraces. This unique suspension produced a smoother ride than that in a coach with steel suspension.

The large rear wheels (five feet one inch) helped the coach get out of mud holes, and the smaller front wheel (three feet ten inches) allowed the coach to turn more easily. Measuring four and one-half feet wide and about four feet high, each coach interior usually had an artistic landscape painting on the door, and gold leaf scrollwork inside. Many coaches were painted red on the outside with yellow trim.

A system of relay stations was set up for stagecoaches. Here horses were changed every 10 to 12 miles, to get a 10- to 12-hour rest. A stage could move six to eight miles per hour, and the relays meant the speed was maintained all day. Arriving at the relay, the driver blew a horn, which drew much attention and caused the innkeeper, postal worker, and grooms to spring into action. Changeover of teams could be done quickly, but if a meal was involved, the stop might be 20 to 25 minutes. Post offices demanded stops as well for stages carrying mail.[6]

A Concord stagecoach typical of the period. Courtesy of Peter James, Abbot-Downing Historical Society, Concord, New Hampshire.

The throughbraces might have given the passengers a smoother ride, but the stage lines often dealt with roads that negated the effects of this suspension. Charles Dickens rode in a stage several times during his tour in 1842. The route in Virginia left a great deal to be desired. His coach was pulled by four horses, and held nine passengers, and the bands of leather, in place of springs, were evident. The coach was covered with mud and entering the cabin was a trial. There was only one step about three feet off the ground and no chair to stand on; it was exceedingly challenging for the ladies in their voluminous skirts.

Dickens wrote that the road alternated between swamps and gravel pits. The mire could reach to the coach windows, and some inclines would tilt the coach to 45 degrees to elicit screams from inside. They covered about 10 miles in two and a half hours with no broken bones, just bruises.[7]

Dickens experienced a stagecoach ride in Pennsylvania that was markedly different, traveling from York to Harrisburg. The coach was like "a corpulent giant, a kind of barge on wheels," with 12 people tucked inside. The luggage, including a rocking chair and dining table, were strapped on the roof. An intoxicated gentleman joined them from a rural bar room. He sat on the luggage on top, but slipped off, and was last seen headed back to the bar.[8]

Reed's comment about the plowing method of the Dutch farmers drew this response from farm implement expert Paul Wood.

That [was] a walking plow since the riding (or sulky) plow did not come into common use until after the Civil War. The walking plow usually required both hands on the handles to insure straight rows. Maybe a very strong Dutch farmer could do it one-handed, but I'm not sure why he would want to. The lines (reins) would typically be draped over the shoulder or plow handles and used only for turns since work horses were trained to follow the previously plowed row... A three-horse hitch for a single-bottom walking plow would imply some serious deep plowing or plowing of virgin soil. Typically, only a single horse was needed.[9]

Pensylvania Oct 2 [September 29] 1841. Wensday Morning cold. Have wrode all night in the stage. Meet a grate meney Pensylvania teams from 10 or 15 in a string. Thay stop and on harniss and hitch thare horses to thare wagons and give them as meney oats as thay can eat, but thay must stand out dores. Let the wether be what it will. Thare is but few barnes [compared] to what you see in VT. Som very large stone ones. It is not uncomen to see a bublick house with out a sine of a shed.

Breckfast on a hill that is dug out for cole to the dept[h] of 2 miles. Breckfast 50 cents. It has ben rather Rainey and cold though the day and verry hilley. Supper 37½ cents.

Riding all night in a stage was rather unusual, given the difficulty of driving a team in the darkness. It certainly would have increased the possibility of an accident and injury to the horses and passengers. The normal practice was to travel from inn to inn to give the passengers a chance to receive a decent night's sleep.

Reed's concern for the horses pulling the Conestoga wagons is indicative of his farming and blacksmithing background, where a horse or two could be the most valuable possession for a farm family in Vermont.

The large stone barns Reed observed were popular with the Pennsylvania Dutch. They were commonly called bank barns, as they were often set into the side of a hill, allowing outside access to two levels. Animals were kept in the basement and hay was stored in the main level. Also, a forebay, or projecting upper level extended over the barnyard.[10]

Reed provided very few details about food and the meals he took in taverns and hotels. The experience of other travelers at that time could vary widely. Philip Nicklin traveled through Pennsylvania in 1835 by canal, rail, and stagecoach. He edited a series of letters about his trip that were later published as a book.

Nicklin noted a tavern meal he had in St. Clair, a small village of two taverns, a blacksmith shop, and three or four dwellings.

It was a very fine specimen of a country tavern dinner, and may thus be described. Table cloth like snow; chickens and ham excellent; eggs boiled to a bubble, and looking as if laid for the occasion; coffee, tea, cream, bread and butter to match; and to crown all, young and tender virgin honey in the comb, of a delicate straw colour approaching white, and almost transparent; cheese, and several kinds of preserves. It should be observed, that all these dainties synchronized on the table, giving it a rich, abundant, and most inviting aspect. The company, however, were at liberty to swallow them in any order, and in any quantity that was to them convenient; each person paying for his quota, thirty-seven cents.[11]

On the other hand, Nathaniel Hawthorne was not impressed with his meal at a tavern in Shelburne Falls, Massachusetts, in 1838. He called the tavern "about the worst I ever saw,—there being hardly anything to eat, at least nothing of the meat kind."[12]

> *Thirsday Morning Oct 3* [September 30] — *1841. snowy. I got out of the stage and walked about 1 mile up hill and sat on a stump waiting for the stage. The timber is mostley oak. Thare is some good land in the valey. I have gown about 150 miles from Frederick and still climing mountains. But the road is the best I ever see. It is cdamized* [macadamized] *for 3 hundred miles.*
>
> *8 oclock. Brock stage wheel and sitt waiting for the Black smith to mend it. Breckfast at Prinston, 50 cents.*

Reed has learned one way to deal with the cramped quarters in the stage. As the stage ascended a hill and its speed dropped, passengers would have a chance to get out and walk ahead to stretch their limbs and take in the scenery.

Here we get Reed's first comment on the improved method of building a road popularized by Scottish engineer John L. McAdam around 1820. The process called for three layers of stone all broken to the prescribed size, starting with the large stones on the bottom layer and smaller sizes for the middle and top layers. The roadbed was then rolled to increase compaction. Side ditches were constructed to aid in drainage.[13]

Turnpikes, macadamized or not, were mainly of benefit to moving people and goods over short distances, serving the communities they passed through, and increasing nearby land values. The roads were not very efficient in the transportation of goods over a hundred miles. For that, the preferred method was via river or canal boats. Tollbooths on turnpikes were avoided at times with bypasses called shunpikes. In addition, the financial backing for the turnpikes with "taxes and stock sales" fell on the shoulders of small investors, causing losses for them.[14]

Pensylvania Oct 3 [September 30] — 1841

Thirsday Noon. Still climing mountains. One [Once] and a while a pleasant vileidge, but the buildings ginerly poor. Nite. Git to the top of the Mountain, one mile above the level of the sea. Supper 50 cents. 9 oclock. Git to Brownsvill. Leve the sage [stage] and the company that I have wrode with from Washington consting of: 1 Jew with 2 [?] [t]housand dollars in 10 [?] ct peaces, one of Mr. Barretts neighbors, 7 men, one woman. Breckfast 37 cents. Rather tired after wrideing 250 Milles with out sleep. 10 oclock take stage for Pittsburg 40 milles. Stage fare 2.50.

No, Reed did not reach the altitude of one mile above sea level. It might have seemed that way, but the highest point in Pennsylvania is Mount Davis at 3,213 feet. Reed was traveling over the Appalachian Mountains that lie in a series of ridgelines and valleys from the southwestern to the northeastern corner of the state. These folded mountains gave him the feeling of constant ascending and descending in the stagecoach.

The mention of "one of Mr. Barrett's neighbors" is probably a reference to Reuben Barrett, who sold Reed approximately 34 acres in Essex, Vermont, on October 8, 1838.[15] This would not be the only time Reed met a fellow Vermonter; he took pleasure in noting all of them he encountered in Ohio. Was Reed's notation of the Jew with money another cultural benchmark for him? He was propagating the stereotype of the Jewish people as rich and covetous, much the same way as when he remarked that African Americans in Washington, D.C., were seemingly enjoying themselves as they strutted about with cigars in their mouths.

Brownsville, Pennsylvania, strategically located, allowed people and goods headed west to access the Mississippi watershed. Perched on the banks of the navigable Monongahela River that flowed north to Pittsburgh and formed the Ohio River with the Alleghany, Brownsville was also on the National Road on the west side of the Appalachian Mountains. Reed's trying travel by stage of ascending and descending the heights of Pennsylvania was soon over.

The bridge across Dunlap's Creek in Brownsville carried the
National Road and was completed in 1839. It was the first
cast iron bridge built in this country and is still in use today.
Painting by Carl Rakeman, United States Department of
Transportation, Federal Highway Administration.

*Rainey as I should have walked. Brownsville is quite a large vileidge. 13 mile
stop ove[r] house, Rather poor land, all oak, oak bordes on the buildings. The
land is mountainous but lies in swells. Quite large wheat fields, it is offen to see
it stack[ed] in the fields, and you will verry offen see them threshin in the fields.
At Noon we took in 3 girles, one from VT, a schoolteacher. Went 20 miles of
the wirst road I ever traveled.*

Pittsburgh Oct 3-4 [1-2], 1841

*Verry poor land, soil about 10 to 30 inches thick and then you come to Lime
stone. And when you git though [through] the lime ston, you come to ston
cole. You will see on all most everry farm whare they get thare cole. Not but few
cattle to be sean and verry few sheap. Thay use thare land to rais wheat.*

*5 oclock, git in site of Pittsburgh. It is a curiosity to traveal down the Alegany
Mountan to the River. The rode windes along the side of the mountain for
about 2 milles. You have a fare vew of the Cittey as you pas down the mountain. It is quite a large plase, but verry Black, a continuel cloud of smock rises
in concequence of the coal thay use. It is so black and smokey that you can
hardely read the sines on thare shops.*

Reed was mistaken about the type of coal mined in this part of Pennsylvania;
he thought it was stone coal, also known as anthracite coal. The coal taken out of
the ground in western Pennsylvania was bituminous, not anthracite. It was superior
for making coke for use in iron blast furnaces. It was also used for heating and light

industries. Since the coal was cheap, plentiful, and easy to access, the sky was filled with smoke throughout the area.

Pittsburgh had an 1840 population just over 21,000. Charles Dickens had this reaction to the city: "Pittsburg is like Birmingham in England; at least its townspeople say so. Setting aside the streets, the shops, the houses, wagons, factories, public buildings, and population, perhaps it may be. It certainly has a great quantity of smoke hanging about it, and is famous for its iron-works … It is very beautifully situated on the Allegheny River, over which there are two bridges; and the villas of the wealthier citizens sprinkled about the high grounds in the neighbourhood, are pretty enough."[16]

After his arrival in Pittsburgh in 1835, Philip Nicklin expressed his observations. "The sensation on entering Pittsburgh is one of disappointment; the country through which you have come is so beautiful, and the town itself so ugly. The government of the town seems to have been more intent on filling the purses, than providing for the gratification of the taste, or for the comfort of its inhabitants. As for the Pittsburghers themselves, they are worthy of every good thing, being enlightened, hospitable and urbane." The industry has been "lauded, supports a vibrant economy and fills this toiling town with noise, and dust, and smoke." You can't blame him for his sour mood—it had taken sixteen hours to go the last 67 miles.[17]

One of the horse begins to fale, agowing down the mountain. Cros over the Ohio River on one of the Nicest Bridges I ever see in to the Cittey. Stop at the stage house and the horse is down on the ground before the driver is gowing Cole [call] for supper. I am watch[ed] by a large company at the table. Git through eating and gow to the sitting room, and hear them in the barroom stateing, "Well, that yankee, how he come hear in the stage?" "No," sais one. "If he a yanke, he['s] a pedler."

I soon have a man in the sitting room. I was reding the news, but he comenced talking and said, "Well friend, I think you are from the east." I answer him, "Yes, I am A yankey." He soon gows out to the Room and tells them he was write, that I am a yankey and I presantly have company enough. But am to tired to sit up long to convers with them, it being the 3d nite since I have slep anney, onley in the stage. Gow to bed and have a good nites rest.

A failing horse was one more challenge travelers faced of this time. It demonstrates the importance of taking on a fresh team on a regular basis.

Reed mentioned a bridge located where the Smithfield Street bridge over the Monongahela River now stands. The covered bridge that Reed saw was built in 1818 and was 1,500 feet long, with spans of 188 feet, and tollbooths at both ends.

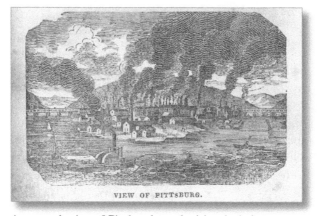

VIEW OF PITTSBURG.

A very early view of Pittsburgh emphasizing the industry, pollution, and river traffic. The covered bridges are evident in the distance. The woodcut was printed in an 1839 school geography book.

This first bridge into Pittsburgh was destroyed by the April 1845 fire that swept across the city and left damage in the millions of dollars.

The definition of a Yankee can take on many forms, depending upon one's geographic reference, as best humorously illustrated by author E. B. White:

> To foreigners, a Yankee is an American.
> To Americans, a Yankee is a Northerner.
> To Northerners, a Yankee is an Easterner.
> To Easterners, a Yankee is a New Englander.
> To New Englanders, a Yankee is a Vermonter.
> And in Vermont, a Yankee is somebody who eats pie for breakfast.[18]

For these men in Pennsylvania, a Yankee was from New England, the home of early American industry. Traveling peddlers distributed the region's manufactured goods, including tinware (pans and dishes), sewing notions, combs, needles, pins, and clocks, throughout the country. They were enthusiastic participants in the barter economy. They "would swap for beeswax, peltry, wool yarn, maple sugar, butter in tubs, ginseng…wood ash — any backwoodsy product that would sell or swap profitably at the next sizable settlement."[19] Some peddlers took advantage of unsuspecting customers and dealt in shoddy merchandise, giving rise to the stereotype of a crafty swindler. Reed was the victim of this stereotyping, probably based on his manner of speech and dress. The other men in the barroom were pleased to have someone from the east to liven up their local news. Reed's stories of his travels, New York City, and Washington, D.C., were most welcome, even though he didn't stay too long because of his exhaustion.[20]

Frances Trollope characterized Yankees as "delightful specimens of [a] most peculiar race ... In acuteness, cautiousness, industry, and perseverance, he resembles the Scotch; in habits of frugal neatness, he resembles the Dutch; in love of lucre, he doth greatly resemble the sons of Abraham, but in frank admission, and superlative admiration of all his own peculiarities, he is like nothing on earth but himself."[21]

Friday Oct. 4 [1]—1842 [1841] at Pittsburgh

Git up verry erley. It is verry cold. Gow out to vew the plase and ingage pasage for Akron. Gow to the river and fin[d] a steam boat jest redey to start for Bever [Pennsylvania]. *Gow back and settle at the Hotell for supper and lodein* [lodging], *46 cts.*

Git a pease of pie, 6 cts.

Gow on borde of the boate. It is verry cold. Count 46 steam boats in the river. It is quite a site to vew the cittey and coale mines as you pass down the River. But it is verry dark in the cittey from the cole smoke and fog. It is quite a curiousity to see them fetch thare cole out of the Mountan.

Ohio River Oct 4 [1]-1841 [continued]

It is brought in rail Rode cares [cars] *and let down the Mountan with Moshinry* [machinery] *Mage* [made] *a purpose for that. As you pass down the River you will see quite a number of verry good farmes and elagent buildings. And some shanteys whare the Nigrows live, that we should not think fit to stable a horse in. Thare is an oposit side of the river from Pittsburgh. A curiosity, it is the houses on the cide of the mountan built one a bove the other, till thay git to the top of the mountan. Thay are the habitations of the men that wirk in the cole mines. The wharef at Pittsburgh is mage* [made] *of a gradual decent from the buildings to the watrs edge (which is verry low now) and everry few feet staples and rings but* [built] *in to fasen boats to.*

So, Reed did have a piece of pie for breakfast! He was true to his Yankee heritage. We can imagine how relieved he must have been to leave the stagecoach travel behind for a while and relax in some comfort on a steamboat again. Steamers started on the Ohio River in 1811 when the *New Orleans* made the journey from Pittsburgh to New Orleans. Boat building was a major industry in Pittsburgh, where 33 steamboats were launched between 1811 and 1825. Travel on the river could mean dealing with low water, as Reed notes, trees and snags, rapids, sandbars, floods, and river pirates. But for the short distance he was traveling on this steamer, Reed could enjoy a smooth ride.[22]

Charles Dickens also boarded a steamboat in Pittsburgh, the *Messenger*. He wrote about the meager meals, "a great many small dishes and plates upon the table, with very little in them." The only drinks on the table were jugs of cold water. But it was his dining companions that made the most impression on him. "There is no conversation, no laughter, no cheerfulness, no sociality, except in spitting; and that is done in silent fellowship round the stove, when the meal is over." Dickens bemoaned the sameness of the passengers, the lack of "diversity of character." "They travel about on the same errands, say and do the same things in exactly the same manner, and follow in the same dull cheerless round." What a relief it was to have a "loquacious" 15-year-old girl liven up the dining table.[23]

The mines that Reed observed around Pittsburgh in 1841 were close to the surface, and coal, several tons a day, was extracted by unskilled labor. These "drift" or "slope" mines crossed a seam of coal on a hillside. With some simple tools, such as a pick and shovel, the coal was removed and lowered to river level in a cart, then on to a barge. Drift mining, which started in this area in the 1750s, was relatively safe, compared to deep shaft mining that came later.[24]

> *About 10 miles below Pittsburgh is a plase coled Economy. It is owened by a cosiety* [society] *cimalarta* [similar] *to the shkin* [shaking] *quakers. Onley thay allow the men wifes a certin ceason of the year. Thare is about one thousand that belongs to the cosiety. Thay owne about 16 hundred acres of Land and several Factoreys. Thay have quite a viludge, but thare is no front dores to anney of thare houses.*

The settlement Reed called "Economy" was the third location in America chosen by the Harmony Society, immigrants from Germany and followers of George Rapp. Rapp, a Lutheran, preached an ascetic life for his people that included a communal society to promote spiritual and economic well-being. For a time, the society thrived with agriculture based on grain and alcohol produced from about 3,000 acres. Their quick adaptations of technology established their reputation for fine textile production of wool, cotton, and silk goods in factories that used steam for heat and power.

The Harmonists were celibate, but on occasion a child was born into the society. Perhaps that's what Reed meant by men having wives only in a certain season of the year. Reed's statement of about one thousand members was not far off the estimated number of 800 to 900 at its peak. It is true, there were no front doors on the houses, perhaps to maintain cleanliness and privacy from strangers.

An 1841 description of the community stated that Rapp, 84 and with "all his faculties," was still vigorously leading the group. Furthermore, the "peculiarities in their internal arrangements" seemed "strange and singular," but "their habits of industry, morality, and strict adherence to sound religious principles, leading to unanimity and peace, speak volumes in their favor."[25]

Rapp died in 1847, but the movement survived until 1905. Six acres and some of the original buildings were soon acquired by the state and are now administered as the historic site Old Economy Village.[26]

The steamboat passage on the Ohio River was about to end, and Reed would again be traveling by stagecoach as he entered Ohio.

CHAPTER 6

OHIO

eed arrived in Ohio entertained by his fellow stagecoach passengers.

Bever [Pennsylvania] *Oct 4* [1] — *1841. Pas several hansom villiedges on the river. River is verry low so that the boat Rubes on the botom. 10 oclock arive at Bever, 38 miles from Pittsburgh, fare 75 cents. Bever is whare the Cleveland and Pittsburgh strikes the ohio river. Git tickett for Akron in stage, $3.50. Couuld got cared* [carried] *in backett* [packet] *boat for $2.00, but it would have taken 1 day longer. Diner 25 cents. Send home 1 paper, 6 cents. I find in the stage the 2 Ladeys I left the nite before at Pittsburgh. 3 men: one from Pickaway co. Ohio, the best singer I ever herd. It was the man that built the buck eye chare and cared* [carried it] *to New york by the Name of F. W. Kellogg, Cinclevill* [Circleville, Ohio]. *One by the Name of Day, a Merchant from Ravanah* [Ravenna, Ohio]. *3 as Jolley fellows as I have met for some time. Supper 37 cents.*

And the Ladys were qite lively and I injoied the company verry well.

Reed's mention of "the Cleveland and Pittsburgh" and continuing by packet boat is a reference to the Pennsylvania and Ohio Canal that was completed in 1840. The canal ran from Akron along the Cuyahoga and Mahoning rivers to a junction with the Beaver and Erie Canal near New Castle, Pennsylvania. It served as part of a water connection between Cleveland and Pittsburgh. Rejecting a longer travel time by packet boat, Reed chose to take the stage for the final leg to Akron.

He was anxious to get to Nathaniel and his family without further delay.

One man Reed met on the stage was Francis William Kellogg, who was born in Massachusetts. He moved to Columbus, Ohio, in 1835, and eventually to Michigan, where he ran a logging business. He represented Michigan in Congress and served in the Civil War. During Reconstruction, he acted as a tax collector in Alabama. From what Reed has left us, it appears that Kellogg took a buckeye chair to New York to participate in some kind of campaign event for William Henry Harrison.

1841 advertisement for the Pittsburgh and Cleveland Line reproduced in the 1914 *Yearbook of the Pennsylvania Society of New York.*

The buckeye chair, along with the more famous log cabin and hard cider, was a symbol of the 1840 Harrison presidential campaign. According to one Ohio historian, the wood of the buckeye tree (*Aesculusglabra*) was "popular for furniture. It's a softer hardwood, and it was very plentiful in Ohio when whites first settled [there]. Hence buckeye wood was a material of convenience, more than anything else."[1] The chair was probably a very simple and rustic design, in keeping with the theme of portraying Harrison as a man of the common folk, even though he came from an aristocratic Virginia family. The Whigs took advantage of a Democratic newspaper's suggestion that Harrison was better off retired in his log cabin with a barrel of hard cider and turned it into the campaign theme.

Campaign workers would pitch a tent outside a town, rally supporters with a torchlight parade, and energize the attendees the next day with speeches, songs, and hard cider. One of these workers had this remembrance 48 years later when Harrison's grandson, Benjamin, was running for president in 1888:

> I voted for "Old Tippecanoe" in 1840, at Mount Vernon, Knox County, Ohio. It was my first vote, and if I live till November, will vote for his grandson because he is a grand, good man. I was a hard worker in that campaign, not as a speaker, but as a singer, log cabin builder, and buckeye chair maker. Ohio being the "Buckeye" state, all the big speakers who came along had to have buckeye chairs to sit on. The campaign was the grandest this country has ever known, and one of the factors that made it so successful was the great number of songs, the glorious Tippecanoe songs, that were sung everywhere. Signed, D. W. Thomas, Pure Air, Missouri.[2]

Another clue about the role of the buckeye chair comes from a mock contest between various factions of the Harrison campaign. Which state would give the greater percentage of its votes to Harrison and his running mate Tyler? A voting challenge between the Harrison supporters of the Strait-Out Club of Ohio and the Ladies of Tennessee (who would award a "splendidly ornamented flag" of that state) and the Ladies of Kentucky (who bet an elaborate barbecue) led to some good-natured kidding. The Ohio club expressed the greatest "adoration for the fairer and better half of humanity," and offered a "full length portrait of General Harrison…and a Buckeye chair with the bark on, a seat fit for more than an empress—the work of a native Buckeye Strait-out Harrisonian mechanic."[3]

The theme of using the buckeye tree extended to several other symbols of the Harrison campaign. A rally held in western Pennsylvania included a parade where "each officer…provide[d] himself with a buckeye cane as a badge of authority… an inventory taken showed the number of buckeye canes carried in the delegation to be 1,432, and…over 100 strings of buckeye beads were worn by a crew of young ladies dressed in white."[4]

The Harrison operation was "the first great political marketing campaign that mythologized a candidate," and was extremely successful, as demonstrated by the outcome.[5] Harrison's opponent Martin Van Buren was seeking a second term, but he was very unpopular due to the economic depression. Harrison and Tyler won by a margin of 6 percent of the popular vote and garnered 80 percent of the electoral vote.

Reed Brown was certainly aware of the significance of the buckeye chair and the other symbols of the Harrison campaign. The Vermont Whig Party had held their state convention in Burlington in June 1840. The parade was a grand spectacle of perhaps "twelve thousand participants," including a replica log cabin, bands, and delegates noted with banners from each county in the state.[6] In addition, the Chittenden County Whig convention was held in Eagle Hall in Reed's hometown of Williston on July 9.[7] Given Reed's habit of reading the newspapers, it would have been hard for him to be ignorant of all the campaigning. There is not much evidence to speculate on Reed's political leanings. However, one clue is the fact that he named his first son Jackson, who was born during the second term of Andrew Jackson's administration. On the other hand, if Reed was like most Vermont voters in 1840, who gave their support to Harrison (60 percent) and elected an all-Whig Congressional delega-

William Henry Harrison, president for just 32 days in 1841. His vice president, John Tyler, became president after Harrison's death. Library of Congress.

tion, he probably voted in the same fashion.

One other "jolley fellow" Reed met on the stage was merchant Henry Lewis Day. Day migrated to Ravenna, Ohio, in 1835 from Massachusetts. He was employed by Seth Day for a while, and later partnered with his brother, Ralph Day.[8] The H. L. Day and Company general store advertised Albany stoves "for sale cheap for ready pay or produce," dry white lead or lead in oil, "Tea…called the best in town," five-dollar overcoats to keep your shoulders warm in winter, nails and glass, boots and shoes, hoods and bonnets.[9] Reed later gave this Ravenna store some of his business.

Francis W. Kellogg, one of the "jolley fellows" Reed met on the stagecoach headed to Ohio. Wikipedia.

The interesting and entertaining people Reed met on the stage ride probably took his mind off the physical discomfort so characteristic of stagecoach travel. A letter in an 1848 Vermont newspaper by "R.V.M." describes stage travel in this part of Ohio, from Cleveland to Franklin in Portage County. It was a section of the state cursed with

> poor coaches, poor roads, miserable drivers, and an entire want of accommodation … The lower part of the coach is constructed like an Indian canoe, and like that "carry-all" you will find it very difficult to keep your balance. The heat was intense and a cloud of hot dust was constantly rolled into our faces, almost suffocating — enlivened it is true, every now and then, by severe jolts and thumps, as the stage dashed through holes, over bogs and rails without a shovel full of dirt on them. I am told that on these same roads in the spring, the hubs roll on the ground while the spokes of the wheel underneath are out of sight.

It was a roundabout route that should have been 30 miles but was extended to 40 miles due to picking up passengers and delivering mail.[10]

Charles Dickens gave travel by stage in Ohio a mixed review. The 120 miles from Cincinnati to Columbus on a macadamized road was a "rare blessing!" They moved along at about six miles per hour in a large mail coach, with a dozen passengers. It was "very clean and bright…nearly new." The stops at the "dull and silent" inns to water the horses revealed that there was no one there to help. Changing the team could take time because of the need to break a young horse, catch him, and harness him, often leading to "kicks and violent struggle." Sometimes the inn owner came out and just watched, "indifferent" to the action. The changes in coach drivers did not produce any variation in their outward character. They were "dirty, sullen, and taciturn," and revealed no wit with answers in "monosyllables." They were weary of the road and made no comments on what was passing. Their "business [was] with the horses," not with the passengers. The constant tobacco chewing and spitting created problems for the passengers, depending on the wind direction.[11]

> *At 2 oclock I got to Ravanah whare the Jale is, from thare to stow corners 10 miles. Then left the stage and started afoot for Akron, 9 miles, got thare jest after sunrise and inquired for Nathaniel Brown. Was informed that he was at Revanah Jale.*

> *Akron, Ohio Oct 5* [2] *1841. Found Melinda and Nathaniels children all well. And that Nathaniel was in Jale on a state warent for braking open a trunk* [in a grocery store] *in company with Sidney Wells.*

It is not clear whether Reed knew where Nathaniel was when he first arrived, but he soon found out. He had arrived in Akron to pursue the second goal of this journey: to get his younger 25-year-old brother out of jail and back to Vermont.

Nathaniel Brown, born in 1816, was possibly the third child of John and Mary Briggs Brown. Reed was the oldest, born in 1810; daughter Mary was born in 1813. The only statement found that connects Reed and Nathaniel as brothers is in a bankruptcy file: "The petitioner [Nathaniel] is at work for his father, John Brown, Jr. [Reed's father], in a blacksmith shop in Richmond [Vermont] aforesaid, commenced in March 1842." The father-son relationship between John and Nathaniel could have been biological or adoptive.[12]

According to Williston, Vermont, town records, Nathaniel and his wife Melinda were married on December 19, 1835. But other information on this family is sketchy. The 1850 United States census shows Nathaniel and Melinda's ages, as well as the names and ages of six children; this information is not noted in the Williston records. In addition, a death record for Nathaniel has not been located.

Sidney Wells, in jail with Nathaniel, was also from Williston. The Wells family and the Browns were connected in several ways. Merrick Burton/Burden, Reed's cousin, married Adaline Wells and was settled in Akron by at least 1835.

Sidney and Nathaniel were in the Portage County jail in Ravenna because Akron, in Summit County, did not have one. The two-story Ravenna jail was constructed in 1837 with "grim, solitary" cells "sufficient to deter men from the commission of any crime, punishable by incarceration within their walls." Twelve cells, eight by six feet, were "formed of dressed Stone" with walls two feet thick. It was built to last, and it did; it was demolished in 1960.[13]

Summit County was created in 1840, so the county offices were placed temporarily in existing buildings. The courthouse and jail, slated for completion by July 1, 1843, were planned to be "similar in construction, and equal in value, to those at Ravenna."[14]

An 1857 photo of the southside of Main Street in Ravenna with the Portage County courthouse (left) and the 1837 jail where Nathaniel Brown and Sidney Wells were held. Portage County Historical Society.

[Saturday, October 2] *Could not eat but a little Breckfast. Went see Esq. Bliss. He informed me that Nathaniel would git acquitted, and then started afoot for Ravanah 19 miles. Took the toe path. Went about 10 miles and my feet began to be verry sore, but I could not git a chance to Ride. Went about 15 miles and coled for supper, but was so tired I could not eat, but put 3 or 4 crackers in my pockett and starte [on] for Ravanah. Supper 12½ cents. Verry tired and my feet so sore that I could not hardley walk. Had to stop verry offen to rest, but Nathaniel was onley a few miles ahed and was very ancious to see him. I got to Ravanah about 5 oclock and found the Jailor gown, but went and got aborder to gow in with me. Went in though the first dore and found all of the inmates confined in the cells. Went up to the upper cells and came to the dore of one and herd Nathaniel Exclame, "Good god, thare is Reed!" and met me at the dore, but had to sit down on his bed, for he was overcome. Staid to converse with him about 15 or 20 minuetts.*

Reed was traveling along the towpath of the Pennsylvania and Ohio Canal when the limitations of his footwear, his hunger, his emotional state, and his need to find Nathaniel all exhausted him.

HON. GEORGE BLISS.

Esquire George Bliss was a native of Jericho, Vermont, a neighboring town to Reed's Essex and Williston. He was born on January 1, 1813, and migrated to Ohio in 1832. He studied law in Akron, practiced there, and served as mayor in 1850. He was a judge in the Court of Common Pleas and represented Ohio twice in Congress. He was "shrewd, logical, and profound; in private life, sympathetic, social, genial, and witty." It is possible that Esquire Bliss took on Nathaniel and Sidney's case when he heard that two fellow Vermonters were in trouble.[15] Samuel A. Lane, *Fifty Years and Over of Akron and Summit County* (1892).

And tride to have the Jaler lock me in to the cell with Nathaniel & Sidney, but he would not, and told me that as tomorrow was Sunday, I could have time to visite them. As I was gowing out, John B. Morse caled to me and wanted to see me. I went to his cell, but the Jaler was in to much of a hurray to let me stay long I then left the Jale and went to the tavern, compleately tired out. Thare was a bunck in the bare [bar] room with 2 buffalow skins on it and I lade down, and was verry soon a sleep for I had not slep but one nite in four and had rode about 5 hundred miles. I slep about 1 houre and the land lorde awoke me to supper but I could not eat enny. I then caled for a bed and it was the hardest wirk I ever done to get up [to the] chamber and my feet ware so swelled I could not hardely git my Boots off. I had walked 28 miles that day, which I think is the fursiest [farthest] I ever walked in one day. I got in to bed and had an ague fit and it was som time before I could stop my teeth from chatterin. Did not Rest verry well. It was a verry pleasant nite, and everry time I looked out the window Who think him inicent of the crime that he is in Jale for. Take off my Bootes and my feet are blisterd a good deal.

John B. Morse was a witness to the crime that Nathaniel and Sidney were accused of, breaking in to a grocery store. He played a pivotal role in the trial.

All of Reed's stress resulted in what he called an "ague fit," bringing on shivering, chills, and perhaps pain in his joints and bones. Directly west of the jail was the Prentiss House, the tavern where Reed most likely spent the night, since it was the only accommodation in Ravenna in 1841.

There seems to be a gap in Reed's recounting of his first few days in the area. He does not mention what he did on Sunday, but the implication is that he spent more time with Nathaniel and Sidney.

Monday morning, Oct. 8. [4] Got to see Esq. Bliss, but he is gown. Gow and get shaved at the [Hotel?], 10 cents. Gow back to melindays [Melinda's] at Noon, Esq. Bliss gits home. Gow and see him and find he is from Jerico Vt. And sais he thinkes thare is no doubt but what the boys will git clear. He wants I should go to Cleaveland and see what proof I can git of Nathaniels being thare at the time the trunk was broken open at Akron. Gow to Nathaniels and Write home, then start for Cleveland. Gow one mile rite out of my way and then start on the rite corse. And tak a canal Boate and find the captan to be at a Vter [Vermonter]. Supper in home stile. Gow to bed and have a good nites rest.

Reed was traveling on the Ohio and Erie Canal, which ran from Lake Erie at Cleveland to Akron, then all the way south to the Ohio River. Completed in 1832, the entire length was 309 miles. The first section of the canal, from Cleveland to Akron, opened on July 4, 1827. Forty-four locks were constructed along this 38-mile span.

The portage between the Cuyahoga and Tuscarawas River watersheds was chosen for the canal route because there was enough water to keep it operable. Before the canal came through, there was very little settlement in the area; Middlebury was the largest nearby town. Akron grew because of the canal, and industries were established there to take advantage of the water power generated by the 149-foot drop on the north side of the summit. In the early 1840s, Akron became the site of several flour and woolen mills that exploited the water power and ease of shipping on the canal.[16] Towns such as Akron, with industries that prospered along the canal, remained viable after the arrival of the railroads that provided a faster, cheaper, and year-round mode of transport.

Akron, c. 1856, insert from *Map of Summit County, Ohio*. The Ohio and Erie Canal runs north and south; the Pennsylvania and Ohio Canal branches to the east. Library of Congress.

With the completion of the canal, products could be transported north to Lake Erie, then to the markets in the east via the Erie Canal through New York State. The alternative was to ship south to the Ohio River, and eventually to New Orleans. Some of the freight included agricultural products, fish, iron, timber, stone, salt, and whiskey.

AKRON IN 1841

"In 1841, a view of Akron from the slope west of the Ohio Canal shows but little building in that direction. There are the business houses around Hall's Corner and along the Pennsylvania and Ohio Canal, the Universalist Church on the left, the Congregational Church on the right, and a few houses straggling up the hill, and east on Market Street."[17] The 1840 population of Akron, at 1,664, would increase 96 percent to 3,266 by 1850.

In 1843, Horace Greeley visited Akron (estimated population 2,500) and noted a mixture of activity in a thriving town, including "five woolen factories, an extensive blast furnace, a card manufactory, nine dry goods stores, and about as many other stores, two weekly newspapers, four large flouring mills, a court house, four churches, and two more being erected. The present water-power, including the surplus water of sixteen locks on two canals, is adequate to impelling sixty-two runs of [mill] stones."[18]

Cascade locks on the Ohio and Erie Canal in Akron, 2016. Photograph by the author.

Don Getz's "Spring in 1877" canal mural displayed by the Cascade Locks Park and Mustill Store Museum in Akron, Ohio. This scene takes place 36 years after Reed's visit; it portrays the activities around the locks and mills so important to Akron's economy. Courtesy of the Cascade Locks Park and Mustill Store Museum.

Reed was on his way to Cleveland to establish an alibi for Nathaniel.

> *Tusday Oct 9.* [5] *Verry pleasant but verry cold and verry hard frost. The land is rather low and swampey. The timber is mostley Buternut and white wood. Name of the boat* **D. Adams,** *fare $1. Got to Cleveland about 1 oclock. Cleveland is a very hansom plase. A grate deal of Busines don thare. Gow to the sadlers shops and find by Mr. Whitelaw.* [Says] *that a man answerin Nathaniels discription was at his shop on the 4 day of June, the time stated that the trunk was broken oben. Vew the cittey and try to git pasage home to Akron, but cant till 5 oclock. Went to see the fire men train. Thare was 5 companys of them. 6 oclock start for Akron on a line boat, verry hevey loded. Gow to the first lock and then git off the Boate and run to catch up with the Pockett* [packet boat] *that had jest past. Have to Run 4 miles before I catch up with the boate. Git on to Boate and git supper and pay fare $1. Gow to bed but don't Rest verry well. Verry cold.*[19]

The businessman who helped Reed prove Nathaniel's innocence was George Whitelaw, who ran a saddlery and harness business in Cleveland. Reed's reference to a "trunk" may mean that the scene of the crime was a grocery store that contained a trunk that was broken open.

In 1840, the Cleveland Volunteer Fire companies instituted a disciplined training program for the volunteers with an inducement of $1 for participation. Due to a lack of a municipal water system, the drills were held at such places as cisterns and along the Ohio and Erie Canal. The training that Reed watched probably involved the firemen pumping their engines and taking water by suction and sending it through a riveted leather hose extended by the hose company. The ladder company practiced placing ladders against a building. The monthly drills were dependent upon agreeable weather. To show off, the volunteers paraded their flower-decorated engines through the streets.[20]

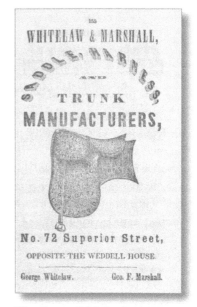

The "verry hevey loded" line boat on which Reed booked original passage was designed to carry both passengers and cargo. It was traveling at too slow a pace to suit Reed, so he sprinted ahead to catch a packet boat that had gone past. Line boats, operated by a transportation company or "line," could be up to 80 feet long and were "pulled by only two animals instead of three, which made them slower" than a packet boat. The inconvenience of

The George Whitelaw business had become the Whitelaw and Marshall Saddlery by the time this advertisement was printed in *Peet's General Business Directory of the Cities of Cleveland and Ohio, 1846-47.*

accommodations on a line boat reduced the cost of passage and appealed to those trying to save some money. Later Reed covered the entire length of the Erie Canal on a line boat as he headed back to Vermont.[21]

Wensday Morning Oct 10 [6] — 1841. Git to Akron, to Breckfast. A lonsom and long day, spent it in vewing the vileidge and boats as thay pas through the lock. Converseed with severall men, ull think Nathaniel inicent.

Thirsday Oct 11. [7] Start for Revanah. Verry Pleasant. Arive thare at Noon. Find Nathaniel feling verry well, stay as long as the turn key will let me. Paid for oats for horse 12½ cents. Git back at suncet, verry tired, pay for hors, $1.00.

Akron Oct 12 [8] 1841 Friday Morning

Went to Middlebury to see Judge Sumner. Find him to be a Vermonter and a verry socible man. Sais thare was not Proof enough to bind the boys over to cort. But Esq. Howard said he thought thare would be by the time the corte sits. He advised me to ceap [keep] still till Burton gits home from Vt. I like the Land south of Middleburry: the bes of enny I have seen in Ohio. The timber is mos-

tley oke. It is quite offon to see large beas [piece] of oak timber girdled and left standing and some times corn planted amonst it. Git back about Noon and gow and git Burtons horse about 9 miles. Take her to Batemans shop to git her shod, but he was gown and I shod her. Evening: went to meeting to hear a Colomite [?], had a tooth ake all the evening.

The Honorable Judge Charles Sumner was born in Roxbury, Massachusetts, in 1794, but the family moved to Townshend, Vermont, when he was very young. He came to Middlebury, Ohio, in 1817. He was active in the clothier trade, a Baptist minister, and a stockman in Springfield, Ohio. Sumner served as an associate judge for Portage County (Ravenna), then did the same for Summit County until his death in 1845.[22]

The Honorable Charles Sumner. Samuel A. Lane, *Fifty Years and Over of Akron and Summit County* (1892).

Here Reed first mentions Merrick Burton, who was very helpful as Reed stayed in Akron. Burton's mother, Betsey Brown Burton, and Reed's father, John, were siblings, making Reed and Nathaniel cousins to Merrick Burton. Merrick, born on June 9, 1806, in Sutton, Massachusetts, was in Akron by 1835; it is possible he was the family connection that brought Nathaniel to the area. Their first son, Wells Burton, born in 1835 in Akron, died at 3 of measles. Their second son, Sidney H. Burton, born in 1838, died on July 4, 1842:

DREADFUL ACCIDENTS. It becomes our duty this week to record two heart rending accidents, that have spread a gloom over our village not soon to be effaced. On the 4th inst. three boys were drowned in the Pa. and Ohio Canal, at the bend opposite the Universalist church — their names were William Gaylord, aged 5 years, son of Mr. S. G. Gaylord; Francis Kidder, aged 15 years, son of Mr. John Kidder; and Sidney Burton, aged 5 years, son of Mr. Merrick Burton. The boys had

Merrick Burton in his later years, findagrave.com.

been playing about the canal with a small raft, and it is probable that all three of them were on it at the time of the accident near the middle of the canal— no one saw them, and the bodies must have remained in the water more than two hours.

It is a sad irony that the success of the canals in the Akron area led to greater economic promise, drawing parents with hopes for the future, but at the same time could take away something so precious as the lives of their children.[23]

The evening presentation by a "Colomite" is a confusing entry. Through mispronunciation and misspelling, Reed could have meant Campbellite, referring to followers of Alexander Campbell (1788-1866), a reformer who broke from the Baptists and sought to create non-denominational churches as part of the Restoration Movement. In 1840, Campbell established Bethany College in nearby Bethany, Virginia (now West Virginia), indicative of the strength of the movement in this area.

Up to 1825, Middlebury was the commercial center of the future Summit County. Stores, mills, hotels, and a population of several hundred people made up the village. Everything changed when the Ohio and Erie Canal began construction in 1825. It was obvious that future growth would take place closer to the canal route, a bit farther to the west. As Horace Greeley had predicted, the city of Akron overspread the region, and Middlebury is now a neighborhood east of the University of Akron.[24]

> *Saterday Oct 13.* [9] *Went to Revanah to see Nathaniel and was admitted with out a garde. Staid 2 or 3 hours. Find Nathaniel feeling verry well, but impatient for the corte to meet. Thare is a grate meney Apples in this part of the contry. Stop and fill my pocketts and carry them to the boys, and some peaches, pares, walnutts, chestnutts & buternuts. Got back at dusk and went and put up Burtons horse at the Ohio Exchange.*

Reed's supplements to the imprisoned men must have been a welcome change from jail food. The Ohio Exchange was a three-story brick hotel on the southwest corner of Market and Main streets in Akron.[25] It was the most popular hotel in the city, and the site of many celebrations during its heyday.[26] Its large livery stable was the home of Merrick Burton's horse.

> *Sunday Oct 15.* [10] *Verry pleasant. Went to the Hotell and found Burtons horse gown, but the landlord agreed to find her. Went to meating, but had the tooth ake verry harde. Had a verry good meeting, subject: the dutey of Universaliss. Speakers Nam[e] Doolittle* [Reverend Nelson Doolittle]. *At Noon was introdused to Mrs Convers. The Universalist have got the Nisest hous in Akron I ever was in. It cost seven thousand dollares. It is carpeted with the nicest carpetin and in sted of slips, thay have settes* [settees]. *Mrs Convers informed me that Price gow* [Grow?] *lives at Newton Falls, about 25 Milles away from Akron.*

Reed was impressed with the First Universalist Church. This stone building, 44 by 57 feet, had a 100-foot-high steeple topped with a gilded ball and "sheet iron weather vane in the shape of an angel." The carpeting and the settees, instead of slips (narrow church pews), were a sure sign of luxury to the visitor from Vermont. Reverend Freeman Loring had arrived in the area in the summer of 1837 to establish a Universalist Society. Dr. Eliakim Crosby, "a man of wealth and great enterprise in business," covered much of the expense of the $8,000 original church building. The Reverend Nelson Doolittle became the second pastor after Loring's short tenure.[27] The reference to Price Grow was probably another Brown family relation, like the connection Reed tried to make in New York City with Wales F. Grow.

Mon Oct 16 1841. [11] *Rainey the fore part of the day. Went and ingaged a man to draw a lod of wood, and went to viseit Mr. Convers. Had a verry pleasant viseit. Mr. Convers sais he is gowin back to VT as soon as he can settle up his concerns, for he thinks he can live in VT as cheap as he can hear and injoy himself agrate deal better. Mr. Convers showed me the grocery that was broken open under the bridge that crosses the conall* [canal].

The original Universalist Church, built in 1837, where Reed attended meetings. Samuel A. Lane, *Fifty Years and Over of Akron and Summit County* (1892).

The Panic of 1837 began a national depression that, "in severity and duration, was exceeded only by the great depression that began ninety years later, in 1929."[28] Those Vermonters who had migrated to Ohio found that, despite the rapid growth in the Akron area, the statewide economy exhibited the same problems as the rest of the nation.[29] It is possible that Mr. Converse saw his future economic security as rather tenuous and decided to spend his days back in the familiar surroundings of Vermont.[30] Reed would later meet several families returning to the east as he traveled on the Erie Canal.

Reed continued his investigation of Nathaniel's alleged crime by looking at the grocery store. It was probably the same store that was described in the local paper with this announcement: Located "Under the Bridge, Between Locks 8 & 9," it was under new management as of May 26, 1841. "J. P. Chapman having bought out [the] grocery store of H. White respectfully informs his friends and the public that he has received in addition to the former stock, a fresh supply, and intends keeping a general assortment of superior articles, which he will sell on such terms that will suit the times."[31] The store was under the Market Street bridge.

Akron Oct 17 1841. [12] Tusday Morning Got up with the tooth ake went and had Doct Howard dig it out.

Wensday Oct 18. [13] Started to gow to the old forge to see Mr. Spafords, but had to Return on act [account] of the tooth ake. Took aswet [atsuete] and it got easer.³²

Reed had Doctor Howard, a fellow Vermonter, pull his offending tooth; without anesthesia, this was probably a painful experience.³³ Atsuete comes from the annatto tree, *Bixaorellana,* a native to tropical America, said to have a variety of medical uses. It is now most commonly used as a natural food coloring. Old Forge was a section of Tallmadge, where a forge was built around 1817, to produce bar iron using a nearby coal deposit.³⁴

Thirsday Oct 19. [14] Went out and got some fower [flour] $1. Paid Mr. Cobb for a lode of wood $1. Went and staid at Mr. Convers over nite: the firs good nites rest I had for some time on act [account] of the tooth ake.

Friday. Oct. 15 Verry Pleasant. Went up to the old forge to see Mr. Spofords. Staid till after diner. Returned and Wrote home. Went to grocry. Got some Aples & Butter and shogar, paid $1. It is sporte to see the Dutch People come to market with thare Produse. Thay ginerly drive 4 horses and ride the near hind horse with onley one line to drive with. You will ofon see them come in to Akron to mill or to traid with not more for a lode than we should put to one horse. It is verry comon at Akron to see 2 or 3 womin come to sell thare Produse with the assistance of a boy to ride and drive the team.

The northeastern corner of Ohio was referred to as the Connecticut Western Reserve, part of a larger land claim by the colony of Connecticut based on a grant from King Charles II of England in 1662. Connecticut sold the property to a land company and eventually it became part of the Northwest Territory of the United States in 1800. Many of the early settlers in this part of Ohio were from New England, now reflected in the architecture, toponyms, and town greens. The "Dutch People" Reed found so interesting were probably from the townships of Green and Franklin to the south of Akron. As Summit County was formed in 1840, these two townships became part of the new county. Since they were just outside of the Western Reserve southern boundary, the early settlers were more apt to be Pennsylvania Dutch than Connecticut Yankee. Some predictions of incompatibility between the two groups were expressed, but over time this proved to be untrue.³⁵ Reed made a similar comment about the habits of the "Dutch People" when he observed their plowing method just after he started his trip from Frederick, Maryland. The education of Reed Briggs Brown continued with his scrutiny of these people as they came to market.

Saterday [October 16] went up to the old forge to see Mr. Spofords. Had a very Pleasant viseit. Spent most of the time makeing saddle tree and blistered my hand in whittlein. Retturned home with tooth ake. Went to the Drugest and paid for Patent--for Melinda $1.

A saddle tree is the wooden foundation of a saddle that is covered with padding and leather. Reed is not clear on where he was staying, but it was probably at Nathaniel and Melinda's house, as he mentioned on October 4.

Sunday Oct 17. Got up erlier than comon. Went and got shaved and got redey for a meating. Went to the Universal meating house to meating. Mr. Garfield Preached a good dis corse and good singing with a man to play on the organ.

Mon Oct 18. Went chestnutting, but did not find onley 3 for thare more hogs than chestnutts on the ground. Went and got Burtons horse. Went and got some Butter, 50 cents.

Tusday Oct 19. Gow to Revanah find Nathaniel rather down harted. Stay about two hours with him. Gow to Day's store [H. L. Day and Co.] and git a pare of gloves, 56 cents.

Got diner, caled a cold check, and 4 quarts oats, 25 cents. Start for Akron. Raines verry hard and coald. Git to Akron at dusk. Gow and get some shogar and ginger, 34 cents. Stop at Middlebury and got screw plate. Took some cold and verry tired.

Reed's dish at dinner was a "cold check," food leftover from an earlier hot meal. The granting of a tavern license required compliance with certain laws. Owners were required to serve travelers food and drink upon request at reasonable times, even if it wasn't a hot meal. One Pittsburgh eatery advertised its 1840 menu of fine Cuban cigars, "pan fish, spiced oysters, ham and eggs, beef steaks, pigs' feet, tripe, sardines, tea, coffee, cocoa, chickens, and very superior venison hams … The above will be served up warm during all hours of the day and until 12 o'clock P.M., and cold checks until 2 in the morning."[36]

Wensday. [October 20] Ground covered with snow. Staid Round in the shops and got some candles, 18 cents.

Thirsday. [October 21] Went and got some hay for Burton. Went about 5 miles and paid 50 cts a hundred ($1).

Friday. [October 22] Rainy and cold. Wrote home.

Saterday. [October 23] Snowey. Went and got some flour $1. See Heasey [?] White. After noon went to carray home girl to Brimsfield about 10 Miles. Verry *mudey. Good land in B*[rimfield], *but rather low. Snow and Raind most of the way home. Got most home and broke out the Wagon fills* [thills]*.*

Having come from Vermont, Reed certainly knew how to deal with the changing of the seasons: candles for more illumination during the shortening daylight and gloves for extra warmth. Brimfield is east of Akron. The thills are the two poles in the front of a wagon that are attached to the horse.

Sunday. [October 24] *Snow abut 4 inches deep. Staid in house most of the* [day]. *Dont feel verry well.*

Monday. [October 25] *Snow about 4 inches deep. Pleasant but cold. Spent the day in Akron Recess, got some Butter 25 cents.*

A "recess" was a combination grocery and eatery that provided customers with access to basic food, along with specialties such as "pickled oysters, tongues, clams, and tripe," as advertised at a Buffalo, New York, "victualling establishment."[37] They were often connected to an inn or hotel to appeal to traveling out-of-towners. The Cornucopia Recess on Main Street under the Farmers' Hotel in Buffalo featured game, poultry, pastries, and "two excellent ball [bowling] alleys to…benefit the health…of customers."[38] In the spring of 1842, J. Mathews & Company of Akron announced a "new establishment" of a "grocery and provision store" on Howard Street where customers could bring in produce to be accepted as payment. Connected with this store was a recess "where may be found the varieties of the season."[39] Some advertisements for a recess often took on an upscale tone, emphasizing the out-of-the-ordinary food, including "a choice stock of Liquors of all kinds, from the most airy kind of light tipple, to the most majestic variety of heavy-wet; selected without reference to cost, and with great care and discretion." The products were the finest and there was "every delicacy an epicure can desire."[40] A recess was an ideal place for Reed to stay out of the weather, read a newspaper, and converse with others.

Tusday Morning. [October 26] *Merick Burton has got home. Spend most of the day with him, it being the firs time I hear from home.*

Merrick Burton, Reed's cousin, had returned to Akron from a trip back to Vermont.

Wensday. [October 27] *Pleasant. Went and got Boots mended. Paid for same, $1.50. Wirk on springs to Burtons wagon. Stop at Batermans shop, got Wood made at Mr. Philops shop, paid for same. 50 cents. I will state hear that I have not seen as much as one shed in Akron to put a wagon in. It is comon to see a wagon wirth $150 staning out in the snow, perhaps once in a while a blankett throd over it. Thare is no sheds at the Publick houses. You will see the* *contry men (as thay are cld* [called]*) come in to Akron and take thare horses from thare wagons and hitch them so that thay will eat out of them. And thare thay will stand in the rain or snow all day whilest the men are drinking in grocerys and taverns. If thay should call for oats for thare horses, thay have a box set up on a poast and thare your horse will have to eat them. It is the same in the Cittey of Washington.*

Reed's spirits must have soared now that Burton was back. He probably asked many questions about the folks back home, and Burton could tell him about traveling to and from Vermont. Reed, no doubt, was anxious to hear all of this, for within a matter of weeks he would face the journey home as well.

Reed was working on Burton's wagon springs, a therapeutic activity for him. He was an experienced blacksmith, and his patent application was for his improved version of carriage springs. He expressed some strong opinions on the treatment horses and wagons received during the day in Akron, and at the same time, noted that the men were whiling away their time with alcohol. His preference for temperance, once again, shows through. It is difficult to determine if he uses the term "contry men" in scorn. His implication may be that true farmers in Vermont would never expose their animals to the elements while they engaged in such disdainful behavior.

Akron Oct 1841. Thirsday. [October 28] *Verry pleasant. Wirk on springs to Burton's wagon most of the day. Paid for turning rolers, 75 cents. ⅜ wire, 38 cents. Wire for springs, $1. Burton went so see the Judges.*

Friday. [October 29] *Verry pleasant. Wirk on springs for most of the day.*

Saterday. [October 30] *Verry pleasant. 10 oclock start for Cleveland on horseback, take the toe path. Git thare about 4 oclock. Went and found Mr. Miller the sheriff, and have him serve surpenia* [subpoena] *on gorge Whitelow. Went and found Ursula Morton, now Mrs. Willson. Took tea with her. Had a pleasant viseitt. She said Tarisay* [Thereasa?] *Wakefieds husband was thare the day before and sais all are well in Mishagan. Cleveland is a hansom plase. Thare is double the business done thar to what thare is in Burlington VT. Put up at the temperance house. Bill, 50 cents. 9 oclock went to bed verry tired so that I could not sleep. At 12 oclock, thare was a band of musick in the street, and I could here the men give the order "sholder armes." What thay were training for at 12 oclock at nite is mor than I now. It was verry pleasan. Most as lite as day.*

The subpoena served on George Whitelaw called him to testify at the upcoming trial as to the whereabouts of Nathaniel Brown on June 4, the date the grocery was broken into. It is interesting to note the role a citizen such as Reed could play in the serving of a subpoena in a legal proceeding.

Cleveland had a well-established temperance movement that began in 1830, long before Reed arrived. People from all walks of life and social classes participated in the effort to reduce alcoholic consumption. They agitated for legislative action to control the production and sale of these beverages that they felt added to the general moral weakness of society. The Cuyahoga County Temperance Society

An advertisement for a Cleveland temperance house. "Whoever wishes for a quiet resting place, and calls on friend Fowler, will find all the comforts of a well regulated Temperance House." *Peet's General Business Directory of the Cities of Cleveland and Ohio, 1846-47.*

was the first of many groups active in this social movement. Some of the groups were formed under religious banners, such as the Catholic Church, and others by fraternal organizations.[41]

It is possible that Reed was treated to a midnight "concert" and drilling of some military group, such as the Cleveland Grays. This was a volunteer militia unit set up to guard against an intrusion from Canada and help local law enforcement. Their name reflected the color of their uniforms. They became part of Ohio infantry units during the Civil War.[42]

Reed's observation, "Most as lite as day," confirms the effect of the full moon on October 30, 1841, and may imply his unfamiliarity with sleeping in a town with oil-fired street lamps. He made the same comment when he arrived in Philadelphia at midnight.

Cleveland Ohio Oct [31] *1841. Sunday. Verry pleasant. Start for Akron. Went to New burgh, a first Rate contry. Thare I found Henry Whipple. Stop in the street and conversed with him about one hour for he new me. He is ceaping school and Preaching part of the time; he look quite Natural. From New Bedford* [Newburgh?] *to Bedford, whare George Whipple is teaching school. I should not have nown him, nor he could Remember me. Staid about 2 hours with him. He told me his Father was thare the day before and that thay wore all well. From Bedford to Twinsburgh, thence to Hudson, thence to Caingo* [Cuyahoga] *Falls, thenc Akron. I like the contry on the above rout verry well. Some of the first Rate farmes and the best cattle I ever see, mostly Drham Breed. Thare is severa miles of Rail Rode on the rout. It is made by laying oak*

*railes length wais of the road and then croswais [crossways] of it. If it was
not for sutch improvements, it would be all most imposible in a wet time to git
along, eather with loded or empty wagon. The land is mostley clay Muck soil. I
see an oposom and stop to pick up some Walnutts. Got to Akron at dusk, verry
tired.*

Was this diversion from the canal route back to Akron done to meet up with
the Whipples? It is not clear from the journal entry. But it certainly provided some
variety in Reed's travels and a chance to connect with more fellow Vermonters.
Henry and George Whipple were born to Wesley and Elvira Whipple in Williston, Vermont, Reed's birthplace. The family of fourteen migrated in June 1832
to Madison, Lake County, Ohio. Over the years, Henry was a Baptist minister, a
teacher, and a professor of belles-lettres at Hillsdale College in Michigan, until he
moved to northern California in 1871. He continued to teach in local schools, and
eventually opened a store, Whipple & Sons. He served as a journalist at two local
newspapers, and later worked at the United States Mint in San Francisco. He died
on a steamer headed toward Oakland on October 6, 1893. His obituary described
him as "well educated, a brilliant and fluent writer, a good conversationalist and an
accomplished gentleman."[43]

George Whipple, born on November 2, 1813, was a schoolteacher for 50 years,
briefly in Williston, Vermont, and then in numerous Ohio communities such as
Unionville, Geneva, Fairport, Newburgh, Bedford, Chester, and Thompson, where
he died in on January 24, 1894. "He always read a great deal, and was well posted
in the affairs of the day. He was a strong temperance man, often giving lectures on
that subject. In the days of Slavery, he was a member of the Underground Rail-
way."[44]

The Whipple family was the kind of family Vermont could not afford to lose
to migration in the first half of the 19th century. They were "high achievers,"
teachers, and active in the Abolitionist movement.[45] Nevertheless, Vermonters like
the Whipples and other Yankees from New England migrated in large numbers to
Ohio and other western states. The first stop on such a journey was not always the
last. Some, like Henry, moved again even farther west. Fertile farming land was becoming scarce back home, travel became easier with the opening of the Erie Canal
in 1825, and an adventurous spirit drove others. Historian Lewis Stilwell called the
1830s the decade of "the Great Migration" from Vermont. Population growth in
the state was under four percent, and the loss of ambitious citizens became a social
concern, often expressed in the newspapers.[46] By 1850, 14,320 native Vermonters
were living in Ohio, and 52,599 in New York State.[47]

Reed continued his sightseeing, enjoying the farms and the Durham cattle.

Ethan Henry Whipple (1816-1893),
date unknown, posted on Ancestry.
com.

George Whipple (1813-1894),
about 1864-1866, posted
on Ancestry.com. Originally
in the possession of Dellice
Whipple, daughter of Guernsey
Goff Whipple, son of George
Whipple.

These short-horn cattle originated in the northeast portion of England, which includes Durham County. His description of travel on the "rail road" sounds like he was experiencing a corduroy road. The construction of such a road was just the way he described it, logs laid lengthwise to the road, then logs placed perpendicular to form the road surface. This would facilitate passage over wetlands.

Charles Dickens was not impressed with corduroy roads. He described them as "throwing trunks of trees into a marsh, and leaving them to settle there." The jolts from log to log were very noticeable. "Never, never once, that day, was the coach in any position, attitude, or kind of motion to which we are accustomed in coaches." The rough roads had one redeeming value. The driver would not fall asleep, because when a wheel "would strike against an unseen stump with such a jerk" he had to hold on tight to remain on the driver's box.[48]

The trial of Nathaniel Brown and Sidney Wells was approaching, and anxiety among all concerned was surely rising. Reed's conversations with the Whipples from his hometown in Vermont undoubtedly strengthened his wish to get on with the proceedings and head home.

• • • • • • • •

CHAPTER 7
THE TRIAL AND HEADED BACK TO VERMONT

Akron Ohio Nov [1] *1841. Monday. Verry warm and pleasant. At 10 oclock, Nathaniel and Sidney arive to Akron in irons to have thare trial. J. B. Morse and Daniel Mans [?] are thare with them in irons for witness against them. Paid Mr. Robb [?] for a load of wood $1. Paid M. Burton for Nathaniel $100. Let Nathaniel have $18. At 10 oclock, the cort was caled to order. J. B. Morse caled on to testify. His statement contradicted it self and could not plase but little reliance on it as he stated. Mr. Mans [?] statement was more for the boys benefitt then hirt. Got through them at dusk. But the cort herd Mr. Whitlaws statement so that he could return to Cleveland.*

Nite. Rainey. Got liberty for Nathaniel to gow home by gitting Mr. Gillett to stay with him.

Tusday. [November 2] *9 oclock. The trial commenced agane by witnesses for N[anthaniel] & W[ells]. And lasted till about 4 oclock. Thare being about 30 on the part of the boys. And when thay got through, the cheaf Judge arose and stated to the lawyers that thare was no ned of enny pleas and comanded the sheriff to take of* [off] *the irons that wore on Nathaniel Brown and Sidney Wells and let them gow whare thay pleas. But to conduct J. B. Morse and Daniel Mann [?] to the jail in safty.*

Finally, the day arrived for the trial of Nathaniel Brown and Sidney Wells, charged with breaking into the grocery store between locks 8 and 9 of the Ohio and Erie Canal. The supposed break-in occurred on June 4, so Nathaniel and Sidney had been in jail for close to five months. The two witnesses against them, J. B. Morse and Daniel Mann[?], were also in court in irons, indicating they were under suspicion from the start. The statements from the witnesses were apparently more helpful than hurtful for the accused. George Whitelaw, the saddlery shop operator, provided an alibi for Nathaniel by stating that on June 4, Nathaniel was at his shop in Cleveland.

On the second day the judge ended the trial by ordering the accused released. Suspicious of the two witnesses against them, Morse and Mann[?] were led off to jail, probably on the assumption that they were the actual burglars. The long wait was over, and Nathaniel had his freedom.

> *Akron Nov. 2, 1841. Tusday evening. Verry pleasant. Went up to see Mr. Convers. Had a pleasant viseitt. Comeing back, I went to vew the grocery that was broken oben* [open] *when it was most as lite as day, and I could not see over the counter from eather window, but J. B. Morse swor he could see the men be hind the counter. Went to Mericks and settled with Esqs. Bliss and Carter and paid them thare fees for Nathaniel, $30.00. Wels paid them the same.*

> *Wensday Nov 3. Pleasant. Went in to the street and every man I met ware re-joising that the boys had had a trial and ware acquitted. In the after noon, went to Cauuga* [Cuyahoga] *falls with Sidney Wells. Went and got Note aganst Mr. Ingraham in favor of Dobins & Wagoner on Nathaniels act* [account]. *Comeing back, I over took a man driving a yoack* [yoke] *of oxen. And he was sick, and it was two miles to a house, and he could not gow with out setting down to rest and I derent not leve him. Got to Mericks about 8 oclock.*

Reed stopped by the grocery store to view the scene of the crime. His observation through the windows supported the belief that J. B. Morse lied about seeing Nathaniel and Sidney Wells inside the store. Later, Morse was convicted of burglary and larceny, and sentenced to four years in the penitentiary. [1] The legal fate of Daniel Mann[?] is unknown. As Reed walked the streets of Akron on Wednesday he received the good wishes of the men of the town. The visit to Cuyahoga Falls with Sidney Wells sounds like part of the final business to deal with before Reed's trip back to Vermont.

Reed's caring personality shines through with his aid for the sick man. His mention of his cousin Merrick Burton gives the reader a hint that Reed spent at least some of his time staying over with him. It is also easy to assume, since Reed paid him $100, that Merrick was instrumental in supporting Nathaniel and his family while he was in jail.

> *Thursday Morning Nov 4. Snowey. Spent most of the day in packing up goods. Went to the clerk and got two coppeys of the trial of N*[athaniel] *& Wells. Paid for the same, $1.50.*

Akron. Nov. 5, 1841. Friday Morning, snowey, bought spool stand for Polley Ann, 18 cents. Spent most of the day in gitting Redey to start for home. Sold stove to Mr. Gillett for $15 and for his staying with Nathaniel over nite. Carried goods to lock No. 11 and did not git on to a Boat till dark to start for home. Have got on to a Boat: Troy. A verry Pleasant Captain Name Brush. Jest as I was startting Mr. Howard, the man that bound over Nathaniel, gave me a letter containing one hundred and twenty five dollars to carray to Buffalow. Thare was six pasengers, one from Williamstown, VT, on his way home.

Polly Ann, Reed and Electa Brown's oldest child, was born on June 24, 1833, so at this point she was eight years old. Reed's gift was a spool stand, a device to hold thread while one is sewing. By starting at lock 11, Reed saved some time on his journey to Cleveland. There were still 30 locks to pass through as they headed north.

A canal boat company could take you all the way from Cleveland to the Ohio River in 80 hours on the Ohio and Erie Canal. *First Directory of Cleveland and Ohio City.*

The fact that Reed was trusted with $125 is a testament to the reputation he made while in Akron. His connection to another fellow Vermonter indicates a longing for home.

Saterday Nov 6. Coald but Pleasant. Got to Cleaveland at one oclock. Fare $4.14. Went to see if thare was a boat gowing to Buffalow. One had jest left. Went to the temperance house. Got a draman [drayman] to carray bagage, pad him 25 cents. Went to see Ursula [Morton/Willson]. Pleasant evening Went and atended the auction with D. D. Chapman from Williamstown, VT, who is gowing home with me.

Sunday Nove 7 1841. Spent most of the day in watchin for a boat to gow to Buffalow.

Crost floting bridge to ohio cittey. Not mutch of a business plase. Wrot to Joseph Bradley.

Assuming Reed started his canal voyage around 6:00 p.m. on Friday, and he arrived in Cleveland at 1:00 p.m. on Saturday, his trip took approximately 19 hours. Boat speed on a canal could be three to four miles per hour, and passage through a lock added significantly to the total. The boat traveled throughout the night. Reed was accompanied by Nathaniel, Melinda, and their two children, Samantha, age 5, and Sarah, age 3. They had so much luggage with them that Reed hired a drayman to cart it once they arrived in Cleveland.

Ohio City was Cleveland's neighbor to the west, across the Cuyahoga River. It was a separate municipality from 1836 to 1854, when it was incorporated into Cleveland's city limits. The two locations were first connected by river-crossing ferries. The floating bridge at Center Street consisted of a platform on logs chained together, with a section that could be set aside to get boats through. The second phase of the bridge utilized pontoon boats.[2]

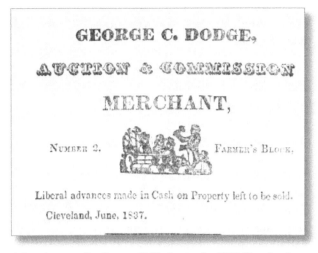

GEORGE C. DODGE,

AUCTION & COMMISSION

MERCHANT,

NUMBER 2.   FARMER'S BLOCK.

Liberal advances made in Cash on Property left to be sold.

Cleveland, June, 1837.

Advertisement for George C. Dodge in the 1837 Cleveland city directory. A commission merchant bought and sold goods for a cut of the profit, such as agricultural products, Syracuse salt, ashes, staves, and stone coal. It is possible that the auction Reed mentioned was carried on by such a merchant.

The population of Cleveland in 1840 was 6,071; in Ohio City it was 1,577, reflective of the significant difference in the business done in each town.

Cleaveland Ohio Nov 8 1841. Sunday nite and no boat yet. Thare is agrate meney borders at the Temperence house and verry stedey, peaceable. No one half drunk and I have not herd one wird of profane language sence I came hear, which is most a mericle in this part of the contry. I have jest herd that thar was a man drowned in the canall. He was drunk and fell off of the boat and was drowned before thay could git him out.

Monday Nov 8 1841. Rainy and two Boats at the Wharf gowing to Buffalow. Pay Bill at books [Brooks?] Hotell $4.50. Dray man 25 cents. Take Boat Consilation. Start at 10. Pay fare $13. Do [ditto] for Children $6. Lake verry ruff. I was so sick I could not walk nor hardley stand. I had to set on upper deck till dark and could hardley git in to the cabin, slep but little. I like the land verry well on the Lake shore, rather low and some swamps. Lake verry low so that the boat rubs some times.

Reed does not clearly state the name of the temperance house that he so much appreciated, but there was a proprietor of a boarding house on Water Street named Mrs. Brooks.[3]

Charles Dickens had a much different experience in an Ohio temperance house that was not to his liking. The water, tea, and coffee all tasted terrible, so he ordered a brandy, but "spirits are not to be had for love or money." He found the practice of forcing unpalatable liquids on travelers rather common, and suspected that the prices charged in a temperance house were elevated to make up "for the loss of their profit on the sale of spirituous liquors." Dickens suggested that these hosts should partake in "total abstinence from tavern-keeping."[4]

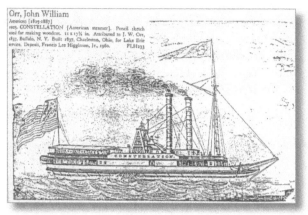

The Great Lakes steamship *Constellation*. C. Patrick Labadie Collection, Thunder Bay National Marine Sanctuary, Alpena, Michigan.

The *Constellation*, built in 1837, was a wood-burning, steam-powered side-wheeler. The wooden hull was 150 feet 6 inches in length, 28 feet 6 inches wide, and 12 feet 1 inch deep. Steamers provided faster and more reliable transportation than sailing vessels, but the large size of the engines took up valuable cargo space. The side wheels on the steamers made them too wide for certain canals, such as the Welland Canal between Lake Erie and Lake Ontario.[5]

The November "verry ruff" crossing on Lake Erie would come as no surprise to those who traveled on these waters at that time of the year. The water temperatures of the lakes are relatively warm when compared to the temperatures of air masses that drop down from Canada in the fall. The water temperatures create a "stationary low pressure" over the lakes that can be amplified by a storm moving along the storm track in the northern United States. In December, the water temperatures are cooling down so the impact of stationary low pressure above the lakes is reduced.

Reed was fortunate that his voyage on Lake Erie only produced seasickness. One year later, in November 1842, a devastating gale and snowstorm caused about 50 vessel wrecks across the Great Lakes. An estimated 100 people were killed. Perhaps the most well-known November tragedy on the Great Lakes was the 1975 sinking of an iron-ore freighter that was recounted in singer/songwriter Gordon Lightfoot's composition, *The Wreck of the Edmund Fitzgerald*.[6]

Charles Dickens took the 500-ton steamer *Constitution*, "handsomely fitted up," from Sandusky, Ohio, to Buffalo in April 1842, with a stopover in Cleveland, "a pretty town." He noted the "high-pressure engines, which always conveyed that kind of feeling to me, which I should be likely to experience, I think, if I had lodgings on the first floor of a powder-mill. She was laden with flour; some casks of which commodity were stored upon the deck." The thin partition of his stateroom caused Dickens to overhear an upset neighbor gossip about the famous author and how he was probably "writing a book bye and bye, and putting all our names in it!"[7]

Reed, along with Nathaniel and his family, were heading home. Traveling on the Erie Canal, the grand engineering triumph of New York State, they saw first-hand the canal's role in the migration of so many people to Ohio and the general growth of the country.

CHAPTER 8

ON THE ERIE CANAL AND HOME AGAIN

elieved to be off Lake Erie with its rough conditions, Reed and his party could enjoy slow, calm travel on the Erie Canal.

> *Tusday Nov 9. Got to Buffalow at 9 oclock. Went to find Nathaniel and Well[s] and went and delivered the letter that Esq. Howard sent to his Brother. Buffalow is a verry Pleasant plase and a grate deal business done thare. Thare was three hundred wimmin of ill fame in the Jale picking ocam* [oakum]. *At Noon start for Albany. At 2 oclock, eat the firs meal of victuals I have senc Sunday noon. Abut 60 pasengers and 350 barels of flour. Nite and we have to lay on the flour* [floor] *and tables.*

> *Wenesday.* [November 10] *Pleasant. Rather low land at Albion. 4 oclock at Brookvill. Horse in ca[n]all.*

Buffalo, with a population of 18,213 in 1840, was truly a major port and gateway to the Great Lakes located at the western end of the Erie Canal. The 363-mile-long canal was completed in 1825, a wondrous technological and physical accomplishment for the time, and a major boost to the economy of New York State. New York City became the major American port in part based on the connection to the interior of the country via the Erie Canal.

Despite the economic depression across the nation, many migrants continued to travel to and from the western states, and many passed through Buffalo. "The dawning of the 1840s saw Buffalo Harbor at its limits of capacity. By 1841 there were 140 lake vessels occupying the cramped lower harbor. A lack of harbor facilities and no means of unloading vessels save for manual labor was the reason for the overcrowding."[1]

Frances Trollope described Buffalo as the "queerest looking" town she saw in the country, with "all the buildings having the appearance of having been run up in a hurry…with an air of great pretension."[2] To contradict the notion that she only saw the negative side during her trip, she made a four-day visit to the nearby Niagara Falls. It was one of the grand highlights of her time in the United States, and left her with "excitement and fatigue."[3] Throughout her sojourn, Trollope was particularly taken by the scenery of mountains, rock formations, rivers, waterfalls, and dark forests.

A packet boat in a lock on the Erie Canal. Jacob Abbott, *Marco Paul's Voyages & Travels* (New York: Harper & Brothers, c. 1852).

If Reed could have afforded the "cheap & pleasant" trip on a packet boat, he would probably have preferred the accommodations to the line boat he ended up taking across New York State. *Crary's City Directory for the City of Buffalo* (1841).

The scene in Buffalo was described by Thomas X. Grasso this way: "Commercial Slip became the epicenter for the lightning swift growth of The Flats and Buffalo following Dewitt Clinton's inaugural journey [opening the Erie Canal]. Warehouses, manufacturers, groceries, taverns, chandleries, restaurants, 'theater/playhouses,' dance halls, brothels, hotels, forwarding companies, lake steamship lines' ticket and company offices, and many other entrepreneurial businesses sprung up eager to serve not only the immigrants traveling west but also the lake sailors and canal boatmen with lively libidos, pockets full of cash and parched throats."[4]

Canal Street in Buffalo, "the wickedest street in the world," was famous for "over 100 saloons and dancing houses, innumerable houses of ill repute and the attendant darker aspects of society which accompany those things."[5] The labor force included numerous men who worked on canal boats and lake vessels. This is mirrored in Reed's statement about the 300 women of "ill fame" in jail picking oakum.

The number was an exaggeration, but the forced task of disassembling ropes down to the basic strands was still used in some American prisons at that time. Instead of discarding old rope from ships, it was painstakingly pulled apart strand by strand, soaked in tar, and used to caulk the seams of wooden boats. The pickers suffered from cut and blackened hands, as well as repetitive strain injuries.

The "women of ill fame" were immortalized in a folk song from the 1840s that has been recorded numerous times. "Buffalo Gals" became well-liked partly because of the ease of pleasing local audiences by simply changing the geographic reference, thus such alternatives as "New York Gals" and "Alabama Gals." "Gal" had extreme negative connotations to 19th-century listeners and was analogous to prostitute. "'Buffalo Gals' was more specifically about those prostitutes that plied their trade on Canal Street in Buffalo."[6]

The 350 barrels of flour on Reed's boat reflect one of the main products shipped on the Erie Canal. Sleeping on the floor and tables was certainly uncomfortable for Reed and the other passengers. They were probably on a larger line boat designed to carry passengers in a forward cabin, and freight amidships. This boat traveled at a slower rate than a stylish packet boat.

But even those travelers on a packet boat could be faced with challenging accommodations. In 1836, Thomas S. Woodcock made the trip from Schenectady, New York, to Buffalo and recorded his experience aboard a packet boat.

On finding we had so many passengers, I was at a loss to know how we should be accommodated with berths, as I saw no convenience for anything of the kind, but the Yankees, ever awake to contrivances, have managed to stow more in so small a space than I thought them capable of doing.

The way they proceed is as follows — the Settees that go the whole length of the Boat on each side unfold and form a cot bed. The space between this bed and the ceiling is so divided as to make room for two more. The upper berths are merely frames with sacking bottoms, one side of which has two projecting pins, which fit into sockets in the side of the boat. The other side has two cords attached one to each corner. These are suspended from hooks in the ceiling. The bedding is then placed upon them, the space between the berths being barely sufficient for a man to crawl in, and presenting the appearance of so many shelves. Much apprehension is always entertained by passengers when first seeing them, lest the cords should break. Such fears are however groundless.

The berths are allotted according to the way bill, the first on the list having his first choice, and in changing boats the old passengers have the preference.

The first Night I tried an upper berth, but the air was so foul that I found myself sick when I awoke. Afterwards I chose an under berth and found no ill effects from the air.[7]

Nathaniel Hawthorne recounted his trials when it came time to bed down for the night.

Wood and canvas berths on the canal boat in the weigh chamber at the Erie Canal Museum in Syracuse, New York. *The Frank Buchanan Thomson* is a waterline reconstruction of a line boat, 65 feet long and 14 feet wide. The boat was named after the first director of the museum. Photograph by the author.

The crimson curtain being let down between the ladies and gentlemen, the cabin became a bed-chamber for twenty persons, who were laid on shelves, one above another. For a long time, our various incommodities kept us all awake, except five or six, who were accustomed to sleep nightly amid the uproar of their own snoring, and had little to dread from any other species of disturbance. It is a curious fact, that these snorers had been the most quiet people in the boat, while awake, and became peace-breakers only when others ceased to be so, breathing tumult out of their repose. Forgetting that my berth was hardly so wide as a coffin, I turned suddenly over, and fell like an avalanche on the floor, to the disturbance of the whole community of sleepers.[8]

With its "greatly restricted" accommodations, self-centered passengers, "tiny berths," and inadequate library of "a dozen books," Frances Trollope could not imagine being imprisoned in such a boat again after her experience on the Erie Canal.[9]

A major concern for Reed, Nathaniel, and Melinda at this time of the year was the approaching cold weather and the closure of the canal due to ice. Mid-December often brought travel on the canal to a halt for four to five months. Boats could be trapped until spring and passengers left to their own devices to continue their journey. Freighters incurred significant extra expense if they had to transfer the cargo from an ice-bound boat to land transportation.[10]

> *Thirsday* [November] *11. Git to Rochester at Daylite. Stay about 4 houres. Rochester is a hansom plase, and thay are building a grate deal. Thay are building a new aqueduct a crost the River. Verry Nise. Had to stop to have the boat weigh. That is done by gowing to a plase whare thay can draw out the water. Got acquainted with Mr. McNeal from Munro, Mish[igan], whare*

Joseph & Stephen Wakefield lives. Start and gow about 5 miles and run a shore. Stop us abut 2 houres. Name of Boat: Highland Mary *of Albany N. Y. Capt. Samuel Parkust.*

"Erie Canal Aqueduct, Rochester, N.Y.," 1855. The aqueducts at Rochester, looking south, showing the second aqueduct, and two arches of the first aqueduct. From "Ballou's Pictorial Drawing-Room Companion," December 15, 1855, 376. Pictures of Rochester and Monroe County, NY, http://www.mcnygenealogy.com/pics/picture. php?/2658/tags/266-aqueduct.

The population of Rochester in 1840 was 20,191, making it the 19th largest city in the country. Much of the economic prosperity of the area was due to the Erie Canal. Rochester had become the "Flour City," a reference to the numerous flour mills on the Genesee River. It was also New York State's largest port on Lake Ontario.

The aqueduct construction Reed saw was the second one to cross the Genesee River in Rochester. When a canal intersected with a river or ravine, it was often necessary to provide a bridge for the canal in the form of an aqueduct. The canal was elevated over the river, along with the towpath. The first aqueduct was built between 1821 and 1823. Leakage brought about plans for a replacement, constructed from 1836 to 1842. The basic underlying structure still exists today as the support for the Broad Street Bridge.[11]

One aqueduct on the Erie Canal has been rebuilt and is operational. It is in the town of Camillus at Nine Mile Creek, west of Syracuse. Using the original limestone supports, a trunk or trough to hold the water was rebuilt with heavy wooden beams glued together, much like the construction of the c. 1838-1841 aqueduct. Photograph by the author.

While in Rochester, Reed noted one of the seven weigh locks on the Erie Canal. At the beginning of the navigable season each canal boat was weighed empty. When loaded with cargo, the boat was then weighed at one of these locks to determine the toll charged. The boat proceeded into the lock, and the water was released so the boat came to rest on a balance scale. The tolls could vary according to the type of cargo, and "the economic and political climate of the moment."[12] For example, to promote the salt industries around Syracuse, the state kept the rate for shipping salt low. Thus, farmers in the west, who used the salt for meat packing, purchased greater quantities at the lower prices.[13] The Erie Canal Museum in Syracuse is in the only remaining weigh lock building in America.

The weigh lock building in Syracuse was constructed in 1850. This is how it appeared in 1907. Erie Canal Museum.

A canal boat registration for the *Highland Mary* owned by John Allen of Gates, New York, April 14, 1838. The New York State Archives. Photograph by the author.

Highland Mary was a common name for boats in the 19th century. It was probably a reference to a song written by Scottish poet Robert Burns about Mary Campbell, his lover, who died at age 23. Burns wrote three works in her honor, mourning her death.[14] The New York State Archives holds a canal boat registration form for a *Highland Mary* owned by John Allen of Gates, New York. On the reverse side of the registration, a note states that the boat was sold on July 7, 1846, and became the *Experiment* in Albany.

Newark, N. York Nov. 12, [Friday] *1841*

[Reed loses track of the days.] *Wensday Rainey. Pass several Pleasant vileidges. For distances on the Erie Canal, I will take them from the towerist* [tourist?]*, and marke them as I am pasing them.*

The next several pages of Reed's journal take on a new format. He reduces the journey on the Erie Canal to mainly a listing of the towns, locks, basins, feeder canals, and bridges that he passes along the way. He starts by providing detail on the mileage from one site to the next, apparently based on a tourist brochure. William Williams produced such an aid in 1827, *The Tourist's Map of the State of New York,*

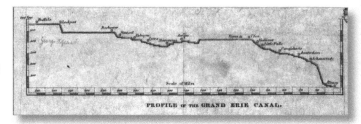

The elevation profile of the Erie Canal from William Williams' 1826 publication *The Traveller's Pocket Map of New York: From the Best Authorities.* Reed's descent from Buffalo (on the left) to Albany is dramatically illustrated, especially the last section below Schenectady (far right). Library of Congress.

just two years after the canal opened. The folded map and text provided distances on the canal from one stop to another, an elevation profile of the canal, connecting stage routes and steamboat schedules, sites worth visiting, comments about impressive aqueducts, rates for cargo shipped on the canal, and a colored map of the entire state.[15]

The cargo rates provide a record of the multitude of goods shipped on the canal: flour, salted beef and pork, butter, cheese, whiskey, beer, cider, gypsum, brick, sand, lime, stone unwrought or roughhewn, clay, earth, leached ashes, manure, iron ore, household furniture, furs, and peltry. Deer, buffalo, and moose skins were charged at a different rate. Also transported on the canal were cotton, pot and pearl ash, mineral coal, pig iron, slate and tile for roofing, timber squared and round, hemp and tobacco, staves and heading, boards, planks, scantling, shingles, and split posts for fencing. Wood for fuel, except that used for salt production, was exempt from a toll. Also listed were the rates for hoop poles and split lath, carts, wagons, sleighs, ploughs, mechanic's tools necessary for the owner's individual use when accompanied by the owner when emigrating north or west for settlement, and cattle and horses.

For the first several days Reed successfully provided the mileage between the towns, even those he passed through at night. But he soon curtailed his notations to just the list of waymarks, spread over four pages. Perhaps exhaustion had caught up with him once again, and he could no longer see the value of listing the mileage between towns if it was already recorded in the tourist guide.

Since Reed provided little detail about his voyage on the Erie Canal, we must draw from numerous accounts of canal travel that provide some reflections on what travelers enjoyed and found wanting as they journeyed between Buffalo and Albany. Given that Reed was traveling in November, it is fair to guess that he spent little time outside the cabin of the *Highland Mary* due to uncomfortable weather.

Travel on the top of the cabin of a packet boat did have a unique danger. Once again, we turn to Thomas S. Woodcock to provide some details:

> The Bridges on the Canal are very low, particularly the old ones. Indeed they are so low as to scarcely allow the baggage to clear, and in some cases actually rubbing against it. Every Bridge makes us bend double if seated on anything, and in many cases you have to lie on your back. The Man at the helm gives the word to the passengers: "Bridge," "*very* low Bridge," "the lowest in the Canal," as the case may be. Some serious accidents have happened for want of caution. A young English Woman met with her death a short time since, she having fallen asleep with her head upon a box, had her head crushed to pieces. Such things however do not often occur, and in general it affords amusement to the passengers who soon imitate the cry, and vary it with a command, such as "All [Andrew] Jackson men bow down." After such commands we find few aristo-crats.[16]

Opinions on the scenery varied greatly, from sublime to horrendous. Nathaniel Hawthorne stated that,

> Sometimes the scene was a forest, dark, dense, and impervious, breaking away occasionally and receding from a lonely tract, covered with dismal black stumps, where, on the verge of the canal, might be seen a log-cottage, and a sallow-faced woman at the window. Lean and aguish, she looked like Poverty personified, half clothed, half fed, and dwelling in a desert, while a tide of wealth was sweeping by her door.[17]

> *Thare is on the Boat 18 children and 40 gown Persons, but we are all very good natured.* [November] *14. Wells sick. Pas through Montzuma swamp, 8 miles long, from one to four wide.* [November] *15. Snowey and cold. Got to Onodagua Lake. Hear thare is acres of land covered with salt wirks. Went and vewed the Rail Rod that pases under the canal. Rather poor contry. From Caricus* [Syracuse] *to Rome 46 miles.*

Sidney Wells, coming back to Vermont with the Browns, apparently came down with an illness. Since Reed does not mention it again, perhaps it soon passed. It is a reminder that canals and other waterways were conduits for the spread of disease. The 1832 cholera outbreak, originating in Canada, spread to urban areas along the canals of the United States, the major routes of transportation in the pre-railroad years.[18]

The Montezuma Swamp was one of the most challenging spots for digging the Erie Canal. As soon as a ditch was dug, it immediately filled up with water. Wooden planks were employed to isolate sections of the digging and hold back the ever-present mud. Nonetheless, the workers had to labor in mud and slime up to their knees. Mosquitos brought malaria to the workers, killing some. [19]

At the salt works near Syracuse, wells were sunk on the shores of Onondaga Lake to pump out salt brine. The salt was produced by one of two methods. Salt blocks (boiling sheds) were set up to heat the brine in large kettles over a wood fire (later coal was used) that reduced the water content and left the salt. This method

Western view in the central part of Syracuse.

The Erie Canal ran through the center of Syracuse. John W. Barber and Henry Howe, *Historical Collections of the State of New York* (New York: S. Tuttle, 1846).

could operate year-round. In the solar evaporation process, the sun diminished the water content and resulted in the final product. The solar method was slower, cheaper, and safer, and was limited to the warmer months of the year. Production peaked with nine million bushels in 1862 during the Civil War, when salt was needed for meat, such as salt pork, for the Union soldiers. The Erie Canal was instrumental in the boom of this industry by providing a ready transport method to ship the salt east and west. The salt production industry led the economic growth of Syracuse and the surrounding area.[20]

The railroad that passed under the canal was the Syracuse & Utica line, dedicated and open to the public on July 4, 1838.[21]

Reed called the stretch from Syracuse to Utica "rather poor contry," and Hawthorne concurred. "We were traversing the 'long level,' a dead flat between Utica and Syracuse, where the canal has not rise[n] or fall[en] enough to require a lock for nearly seventy miles. There can hardly be a more dismal tract of country."[22]

> *Liverpool, NY Nov. 14 — 1841* [continued]
>
> *Thare is 3 familys on the Boat that are moveing back* [from] *Mishigan, 2 from Ohio, and thay say thare is not but one in ten but what would move back to the East if thay could git money to git back with. Sunday nite at Utica. Hansom plase. Monday Morning* [November 15] *at Little falls. Stop all day on act.* [account] *of two Boats being sunk in the canall, and we had to wait for our turn in gitting to the Locks. Thare was one man drowned in the canall, he was drunk. Snow all day.*

Some migrants who moved west to such states as Michigan and Ohio returned home for a variety of reasons. With the depression still impacting the country, settling in a new area did not guarantee economic well-being. Lewis Stilwell made the case for Vermont not feeling "the economic collapse as did the western states. There were no longer any wild lands or any other unplumbed resources in the Green Mountains, which could be capitalized into a shaky structure of speculative credit such as was overshadowing Michigan, Illinois, and Ohio."[23] Vermonters contemplating a move west may have put it off for a few years, or, if they were already settled in one of those states, the move back to the east could make economic sense for the families.

Some became homesick for family and friends. Extreme weather and crop failure sapped the confidence of many. Perhaps a family just did not fit into their new environment for religious and/or political reasons.

Moving and settling in the west or remaining in or returning to the east each had proponents who provided more than enough opinions and propaganda in newspapers, travel guides, letters back home, Sunday sermons, and day-to-day conversation. On one side, it was claimed that the land in the west was flat, fertile, and cheap. The climate was healthy and mild. The future was there; growth was inexhaustible. Or you could believe those who claimed the west was marked with poor drinking water, health issues, and "no schools, no churches, no New England morality — one's children would unquestionably grow up to be non-New Englanders — with all that that meant."[24]

One desperate Vermont newspaper played on potential migrants' worst fears: disease and death resulting in "tales of sorrow and sadness." Those who had left New England had "been flattered to sell out a comfortable home, surrounded by schools and good moral and religious privileges," by a speculator, a dishonest cohort, or "a[n] irresponsible cheap Philadelphia or other city paper." The lack of funds kept many from returning to their homes from the west. Using dubious statistics, it was claimed that an estimated one out of two would not survive beyond the first five years. The article granted that some made out okay, "but three-fourths who go west do not [do] half so well as they were doing or might do here."[25]

Utica was a noteworthy stop on the Erie Canal, according to the tourist guides. In 1831, William Williams commented in his guide to the canal that the town, with a population of about 8,000, served as a market for the farms in the surrounding counties. The canal had "greatly increased its prosperity." The "compact and handsome style" of the brick buildings made them "specimens of taste." The inns were "commodious" and "well kept." Outside of New York City, Oneida County was the most populous in the state. "Its prospects of permanent and growing consequence were never so good as at present."[26]

By 1836, Utica elicited this response from Hawthorne: "[We] find ourselves amid piles of brick, crowded docks and quays, rich warehouses and a busy population. We feel the eager and hurrying spirit of the place, like a stream and eddy whirling us along with it."[27]

The gorge at Little Falls, formed by the Mohawk River as it cuts through the mountains, made the Erie Canal

"Bird's-eye view of Utica over Bagg's Square in the 1850s, showing the smoke from numerous factory chimneys." *Oneida County Historical Society Year Book*, 1 (1881): 144-155.

possible. Thus, the Mohawk Valley became the most important access from the populated eastern seaboard to the burgeoning west. As "a point of grandeur and effect," the aqueduct at Little Falls nearly equaled that in Rochester, opined William

Southern view of part of the Village of Little Falls.

Little Falls. John W. Barber and Henry Howe, *Historical Collections of the State of New York* (New York: S. Tuttle, 1846).

Williams. It was 214 feet long, supported by three limestone arches, with the 70-foot center arch allowing passage of the river. "Great taste and judgment have been displayed in the execution of this work. Connected with the romantic scenery of the 'pass of the Mohawk,' it is unrivalled by any other point on the canal. It serves the double purpose of a side cut to the flourishing village of Little Falls, and a most important feeder" providing water to a larger canal.[28] "Canal boats could take this 'siding' into Little Falls or through boats could continue on in the main canal on the south side of the river."[29]

The competition between canal boat crews was legendary. Supposedly, a boat had a crew member duke it out with a rival boat crewman if they were jockeying for the same lock. The tradition of fighting was perpetuated by the folklore and novels written about the canal.[30] Tempers flared when traffic backed up at the inadequate locks, and freight delivery was delayed. Also, sunken boats, as Reed experienced at Little Falls, brought on disruption to boat passage. But what happened on the *Highland Mary*, about a month before Reed boarded in Buffalo, was a tragedy that took the rivalry between boats to a new level. On October 3, 1841, the boat was headed west near the town of Fonda when its towline became entangled with the line of the *J. C. Hawley*. The bowman of the *Highland Mary* jumped into action to cut the line. He was hit on the head by a pole wielded by a crew member of the *J. C. Hawley*, and died an hour later of a fractured skull. A newspaper rightfully called it "murder."[31]

There were numerous other reasons why boat traffic was slowed or halted completely: "aqueduct walls crumbled; locks malfunctioned; and canal banks burst open."[32] Boats banged into each other in the narrow passages, silt could reduce the depth of the four-foot canal, and the traffic jams at locks could delay boats traveling the full length of the canal on average 36 hours in 1842.[33]

> *Schenectady, Nov. 17, 1841. Good land on the Moonholk [Mohawk] River.*
> *Warm and pleasant. Crost the Aqueduct. 14 arches about 45 feet each, making*
> *the whole length about 730 feet of the solist [solidest] and handsomes stone*
> *wirk I ever see. Lower aqueduct: 28 arches, 35 feet, making 980 feet. Got to*
> *the Lockes at the Junction, 12 oclock. Went down to see if I could find aboat*
> *for Whitehall, but did not git though till about 11 oclock at Nite. Went twise to*
> *Troy but could not find aney boat, till about one oclock in the morning. Paid fare*
> *on the Eri Calall $25.63.*

Near Schenectady, the Erie Canal crossed the Mohawk River twice, once on the Upper Aqueduct at Rexford, then again, several miles downstream on the Lower Aqueduct at Crescent. The Williams guide offered these statistics on the aqueducts: the upper was 748 feet long with 16 stone piers and "butments"; the lower aqueduct was 1,188 feet long with 26 stone piers and "butments."

The remains of the Rexford aqueduct on May 11, 2017. Photograph by the author.

What Reed called "Junction" was the point where the original Erie Canal met the Champlain Canal. Juncta was the first name of what is now the city of Cohoes.

Between Schenectady and where the Erie Canal met the Hudson River, there were 27 locks that slowed down travel considerably. Those in a hurry would take a stage, and later a railroad, to bypass this section of the canal.[34] The Mohawk & Hudson Railroad had begun service on September 24, 1831, so it was available to Reed. From his description, we know he stayed on the canal all the way, perhaps to save money and the hassle of transferring one more time to another mode of travel with his charges and luggage. He didn't waste any time in trying to secure passage on the Champlain Canal north to Whitehall. The threat of a freeze over was ever-present as the days of November rolled by. It had taken him nine days to travel from Buffalo to the end of the canal at the Hudson River. The average time for the trip was five to seven days.[35]

> *Thirsday Nov 18 1841. at Stillwater paid for supper, 18 cents.*

> *Friday Nov 19. Got to Whitehall at 1 oclock. Time enough to take the steam boat* Whitehall. *I went 8 miles afoot so [to] git [to] Whitehall in season to take the boat, and lef the canall boat aback about 2 miles with Nathaniels Family. Paid for Deck Pasage on steamboat $1.50. Got to Burlington at 11 oclock and sent Nathaniel $10. Walked home. Got home about 1 oclock.*

> *Saterday Nov 20 1841. Went to Burlington after Nathaniel. Paid fare $9.25. Got home about 4 oclock Sunday Morning.*

From the Erie Canal to the Champlain Canal, Reed continued his journey north. His journal entries reveal his anxiousness to get home. Stillwater, Reed's supper spot, is located on the western bank of the Hudson River. As he had done in Ohio, Reed once again left a canal boat to sprint ahead and make better time. The deck passage on the steamer *Whitehall* was a cheaper way to go versus securing a cabin. This steamer was a sister ship to the *Burlington*, which Reed had taken on the first leg of his journey up Lake Champlain in September.[36]

Reed's continued loyalty to Nathaniel and his family was evident to the end of the 57-day journey. He had traveled about 2,150 miles using all the forms of transportation available in 1841. His approximate expenses were: transportation, $105.16; food/meals/lodging, $19.17; personal (clothes, gifts, haircut, etc.) $40.58; patent, $45.25; trial, $131.50. Grand total: $341.66. Given the familial obligation of Reed's journey, it is logical to surmise that he had financial backing, perhaps from his father and grandfather.

Disappointingly, Reed recorded his homecoming in a totally matter-of-fact way. There was undoubtedly much rejoicing all around. He had mentioned the gift he bought for Polly Ann, a spool stand. He must have brought other gifts home for his wife Electa, his sons Jackson and Bertram, and other family members. The sense of accomplishment was partial now, for he had successfully brought Nathaniel, Melinda, and their family home. The notice of the granting of the patent for his carriage springs came along a few weeks later. The patent influenced his travels considerably in the upcoming new year.

. . . .

CHAPTER 9

EPILOGUE

After 45 pages detailing his excursion, the rest of Reed's journal gives the reader a glimpse of what occupied him for the next few years. Several weeks after returning home, he recorded a trip to Canada to pick up three cutters (sleighs), pay duty on them, and sell them in the United States. On this trip, he was away from home over Christmas.

Reed was determined to make the results of his trip to Washington, D.C., for a patent yield some dividends. His patent for the improved carriage springs was granted on December 14, 1841, and this had an impact on his income later in 1842. On June 28 of that year, he crossed Lake Champlain to Plattsburgh, New York, bought a map of the state, and proceeded to visit towns in the north to sell the rights to his patent. He stopped in Ellenburg, "Shadagee" (Chateaugay), Malone, Lawrenceville, Norfolk, Massena Springs, and Columbia. He did not mention inns or hotels, and seemed to spend his nights with residents, some of whom were former Vermonters he knew. He sold and bartered the rights and accepted a wide variety of items in exchange.

Bartering was a major part of the local economy in northern New York and Vermont in the 1840s. Very little currency was in circulation, so the bargaining parties had to come to some agreement on the value of an item or service. A record was kept in a ledger, with debits and credits noted. Since Reed was dealing with people outside of his familiar territory of Chittenden County, he hoped to settle on the spot.[1]

Reed also accepted promissory notes in lieu of immediate payment. This was a promise to pay a certain amount on a future date. On July 7, 1842, he sold the rights to the patent in the states of Pennsylvania and New Jersey to Mr. Samuel

Ritcherson/Richardson for items valued at one thousand dollars, and received two horses at $200, a harness at $25, a wagon at $30, shop and tools worth $700, and some timber at $45. Reed does not elaborate on the final disbursement of these items. He probably continued his trading and selling until he returned home on July 21. Reed also accepted a brass-covered harness, a wagon, a pair of thin boots, and grain. Watches, especially gold watches, became a common item exchanged for the patent. Apparently, a good number of people saw value in Reed's patent and were willing to come to satisfactory terms with him.

During this trip into New York State, Reed took time to go to meeting (attend church), get his teeth cleaned (50 cents), hear a July 4th oration, and learn of the death of his sister Clotilda on July 5. He did stay with Tiras Hall, the gentleman he met in Whitehall, New York, during his 1841 trip, who wanted the patent for St. Lawrence County. His bartering continued: to Mr. Squares for a watch, and to "Dr. Dunton's son for four towns for an Indian pony." On July 17, Reed went deer hunting.

Reed had a partner in the selling and bartering of the carriage springs patent, John C. Griffin, a Williston, Vermont, native. For example, Griffin exchanged the rights to J. N. Stevens for Orleans County, Vermont, for one watch and a double-barreled gun. The financial records for the years after 1842 are rather spotty, but several notations in January 1847 show that Reed received such things as a lumber wagon, a sleigh, a harness, two whiffle trees, and a neck yoke for his patents. He could have been continuing to sell the rights to the carriage springs, or he could have been pre-selling the rights to his next patent for a drag saw, which was granted on April 10, 1847, or both.

Reed must have had a salesman's personality, someone who loved to introduce himself to strangers, engage in conversation, and make a case for his carriage springs.

Other challenges arose for Reed Brown and his wife Electa in 1842. Reed sold his 34 acres in Essex, Vermont, and moved back to Williston.[2] In September, Reed and Electa had an infant son who died shortly after birth.

Their daughter Jane was born on December 25, 1843, and son Byron on August 17, 1846. By the fall of the same year the family had moved from Williston to Fletcher, Vermont, where, with the financial help of Roswell B. Fay, Electa's brother, they purchased a 300-acre farm on River Road, near the intersection of School Road. The farm encompassed some of the fertile land along the Lamoille River. With a growing family, the Browns decided to try farming on a larger scale; the patents became a sideline.[3] Products from the farm ranged from potatoes, butter, and cheese, to hay, hops, and maple sugar.[4]

With the birth of daughter Edith in 1850, Reed and Electa now had six children. Son Roswell would follow in 1853. After an 1856 transfer, Reed completely owned the farm in Fletcher.[5]

The oldest Brown son, Jackson, age 22, migrated to California in 1857, where he became a successful rancher in Solano County and a member of the California State Assembly. His grand architect-designed Italianate house, still standing, was constructed in 1887 and 1888. "The largest residence in the agricultural district of the county, it became known as a meeting place for church socials, political and community affairs, and family gatherings."[6] The house is now on the National Register of Historic Places.

Reed and Electa's oldest son, Jackson Fay Brown, in California. Ancestry.com.

Reed received patent number 26746 on January 10, 1860, for a reciprocating saw. In November 1866, Reed sold his Fletcher farm to Sumner Carpenter for $9,000.[7]

With most of their children gone, Reed and Electa were looking for a smaller home and a change from farming, and wished to be closer to their extended family. They settled in North Williston, where Electa purchased 7½ acres and a house.[8] Electa had two brothers living there: Roswell B. Fay (on what is now the Fontaine farm) and Hiram. Roswell was the oldest child of John and Polly Fay of Richmond, Vermont. He was involved in farming and lumber manufacturing in this part of Williston. Hiram Fay, the youngest child of John and Polly, also lived in North Williston. He manufactured hay rakes for a short time, and he also operated a saw and grist mill. Roswell B. Fay's son, John M., lived in the Fay farmstead on Fay Lane.[9]

Roswell E. Brown, youngest child of Reed and Electa. He was part of his father's butter tub manufactory for about ten years. From 1894 to about 1933, he ran the general store in North Williston, Vermont. He also represented Williston in the Vermont legislature in 1898. *Legislative Souvenir, 1898.* Special Collections, Bailey / Howe Library, University of Vermont.

Reed and Electa Brown's youngest child, Roswell Brown, also settled in North Williston. Eventually he ran the general store and was a partner in the family butter tub business. Reed and Electa were surrounded by family.

John Brown Jr., Reed's father, died in 1868. On August 23, 1869, Reed sold his father's 130-acre farm to

Thomas Metcalf for $9,200.[10] The farm was located south of what was known as the Winooski Turnpike, near what is now the corner of Williston Road and Tower Lane, just west of the village.

The 1870 Census indicates Reed and Electa were in California with their son Jackson and his family for a long-term visit. The Brown's probably traveled across the country and back on the recently completed transcontinental railroad.

The former Reed and Electa Brown house at 18 Fay Lane, North Williston, Vermont. Photograph by the author.

It would not have been an easy process, changing from one rail line to another numerous times, and often traveling between depots as Reed had done in Baltimore in 1841. *Harper's New Monthly Magazine* recommended that a traveler coming from New York and "bound to California will do well to stop two days in Chicago, and one day in Salt Lake City, in which case he would get to San Francisco in ten days, and with surprisingly little fatigue."[11] Despite the trials of cross-country travel in 1870, Reed must have marveled at the vast improvement they experienced compared to his 1841 journey. Williston resident Lucia Darling implied in her diary that Reed was back in town at least by April 24, 1871.[12]

In the late 19th century dairy farming dominated Vermont agriculture. Along with cheese, butter was produced from large operations and local farms. It was packed into wooden boxes and tubs to maintain freshness, perhaps labeled with the name of the farm. Butter was an important source of income for a family, a real cash crop. A November 21, 1873, announcement in the *Burlington Free Press* stated that R. B. Brown & Son, "having purchased the entire stock and manufactory of Wilkins & Loggins, we are prepared to furnish their improved butter tubs in lots of fifty to one thousand, or by the [rail] car load, on short notice and on favorable terms. Address all orders to R. B. Brown & Son, No. Williston, Vt." The industries in North Williston located there because of the rail line that came through this section of the town, allowing the shipment of products throughout the urban Northeast. Like most of the businesses, the Brown manufactory was located on the north side of Chapman Lane.

Walton's Register records that the Brown family was involved with butter tub manufacturing in North Williston up to 1886.[13] Reed Brown and three of his sons—Bertram Fay, Byron Briggs, and Roswell E. — all had a hand in this industry at one time. In the early 1880s, they employed ten men, manufacturing $12,000 worth of butter tubs per year.[14]

Anyone ordering a thousand tubs most likely was working in a creamery that produced large quantities of butter. For instance, just down the road from Brown's plant was the Smith Wright & Sons cold storage facility that shipped poultry, butter, and eggs on the railroad. Smith Wright used Brown-made butter tubs to keep his deliveries fresh. At one time in 1893, the Wright business had 750,000 pounds of butter in storage, along with more at the home farm a couple of miles away.[15]

An "Elgin-style" butter tub and cover made of ash was pioneered by the Elgin Butter Tub Company of Illinois. Courtesy of Paul Wood.

Hardwood or spruce were common materials for butter tubs. The Browns typically manufactured tubs of elm and basswood, with a small minority made of spruce. Basswood was preferred because it was odorless and did not transfer a disagreeable taste to the butter. Most of their tubs were of the 50-pound variety, with smaller numbers of 30-pound and 20-pound tubs. Of the 34 manufacturers of butter tubs in Vermont in 1878, R. B. Brown & Son was the only one listed in Chittenden County.[16] By 1882 the competition had increased, with nine firms in the county.[17]

The Browns also produced grain measures and oil can jackets, according to a single listing in *Walton's Vermont Register* for 1887. An oil can jacket, also made of wood, protected a can of oil from puncture and the ensuing fire hazard.

This grain measure, made by the Brown brothers, is a four-quart container that could be used to ration out a specific amount of feed for an animal. Williston, Vermont, Historical Society.

Paul Wood, a noted Vermont expert on 19th-century farm implements, explained that the Brown brothers' grain measures were well made and iron reinforced, with bentwood sides and nail fasteners. "Although such devices could measure any dry granulated (typically agricultural) material, a principal use was to measure the miller's portion — the fraction of grain kept by the miller in payment for grinding the grain. Measures could be purchased in nested sets — for example, 2, 4 and 8 quarts. Also, double measures were made —

for example, 2 quarts on one side and 4 quarts on the other… Measures were also made in larger bushel sizes."[18] Another principal use of the measure was to insure accurate amounts of grain during a sale.

Reed, now out of farming and involved in a well-established business with several of his sons, enjoyed a change of pace and an occupation with different demands. The Brown nesting butter tubs were awarded a certificate and an honorable mention at the 1874 Chittenden County Fair in Essex Junction, and a certificate at the 1876 fair.[19]

Reed Briggs Brown gravestone in the East Cemetery, Williston, Vermont. "Mourning for I am with you." Photograph by the author.

Reed's involvement with the business lasted until his death on March 31, 1878, at 67 years, 8 months, and 26 days.[20]

The 1880 Census reveals that Electa was living in North Williston with her son Roswell and his wife Julia. On December 11, 1889, Electa Fay Brown died in Cambridge, Vermont, due to cancer of the stomach, at 78 years, 9 months, and 17 days.

NATHANIEL BROWN, 1816-?

Nathaniel Brown's life story is marked with misfortune, financial problems, tragedy, and mystery. It is not clear whether Nathaniel was the natural-born son of John Brown Jr. and Mary Brown, or adopted. The lack of a written birth record raises the question. His birth year of 1816 is taken from the 1850 Census, when he and his wife Melinda were living in Hinesburgh, Vermont, with their six children. Adoptions in the 1800s were not necessarily a legal arrangement requiring approval of an agency and paperwork. If done within an extended family, the adoption would be much less formal, and not recorded in any official document.

There is evidence that Nathaniel was living in Williston in 1835, for he is mentioned in Hiram Phelps' journal in a John Brown entry, "One hat for Nathaniel, $4.00." On December 17, 1835, Nathaniel was listed again: "John Brown, Dr, to making for pantaloons for Nathaniel, .50." This was in preparation for Nathaniel's wedding two days later.[21]

The December 19, 1835, marriage between Nathaniel Brown and Melinda Brown, both of Williston, was presided over by Chauncey Brownell, justice of the peace and town clerk.

From December 23, 1837, to September 28, 1838, Nathaniel is listed (on three separate pages) in the Reed B. Brown ledger section of his journal with a variety of items: sheep, corn, wheat, oats, apples, sugar, beans, beef, a watch, house rent, shop rent, and a harness. The notation of "lost time" at $1 per day appears on numerous occasions. It indicates that Nathaniel was working for Reed in the blacksmith shop in Richmond.

On October 22, 1838, Reed sold his blacksmith shop and land in Richmond to John Brown Jr., his father, for $600. The transaction was signed in the presence of Nathaniel Brown and Chauncey Brownell in Williston. It is possible that John bought the shop for Nathaniel.[22]

Sometime around 1840, Nathaniel and Melinda moved to the Akron, Ohio, area. They were probably encouraged to make the move by John Brown Jr. and cousin Merrick Burton, who had settled there by 1835. Nathaniel does not appear in the 1840 Census for Akron. He could have arrived after the count. His children at that time were Samantha, age 4, and Sarah A., age 2.

Historian Jan Albers makes a case against the "mythology" that it was just the adventurous and ambitious Vermonters who migrated out of state. If someone was economically secure at home, why would they leave the familiar and risk failure on an expensive relocation far away? "Those who left were as likely to be the ones who had been unsuccessful [in Vermont] as they were to be those with a fire in the belly."[23] Nathaniel certainly fit the definition of a hard-up Vermonter seeking a new start in a different location.

During the summer and fall of 1841, Nathaniel was in jail in Ravenna, Ohio, awaiting trial in Akron. The charges were dismissed, and in November Nathaniel and his family returned to Vermont with Reed.

One outcome of the economic depression that had gripped the country since 1837 was the Bankruptcy Act of 1841. This allowed individuals, not just merchants and traders, to go through bankruptcy, either voluntarily or involuntarily. Nathaniel took advantage of this law to ease the family's financial plight.

In March 1842, "The petitioner [Nathaniel] is at work for his father, John Brown, Jr., in a blacksmith shop in Richmond aforesaid," according to Nathaniel's bankruptcy ruling.[24]

On July 25, 1842, when Nathaniel filed for bankruptcy, he was about $1,507 in debt. He owed money to people in Burlington, Williston, Richmond, Hinesburgh, and Middlebury, Vermont. His largest debts were to his father, John Brown Jr., $336; to J. and J. H. Peck & Co., merchants in Burlington, $226; and to his brother Reed, for cash and sundry articles of merchandise for $200. Reed had been purchasing items for Nathaniel's family.

There appeared, as well, a debt to James Mason, merchant of Akron, for merchandise, with a balance due of about $40. There was also a debt to Doctor Howard of Akron (who helped with Reed's toothache), for medical services for about $30.

On the plus side, Nathaniel was owed $94.01 from eight people, mainly for blacksmith work. Seventy dollars of that total was tied up in a legal case in Akron.

The bankruptcy filing listed the family's possessions, from furniture, one cow, and three cords of wood to the amount of food and crockery on hand. The Brown's "wearing apparel," including pantaloons, dresses, and stockings, was also part of the inventory. It is a stark and demeaning picture of a family on the edge of poverty in Vermont in 1842. The bankruptcy became official on August 31.

The next authoritative record for Nathaniel Brown, working as a blacksmith, and his family, comes from the 1850 Census. He was 34 years old and living in Hinesburgh with his wife, Melinda, age 34, and Samantha, age 14, Sarah, age 12, Oscar, age 6, Lucy, age 3, and twins Theodore and Isidore, 6 months old. Since their family had grown significantly since 1842, perhaps their economic situation had improved. In 1851, Nathaniel and Lewis Dow had a mortgage deed with William C. Benton for land in Hinesburgh and blacksmith tools, two pairs of bellows, one vise, two anvils, three screw plates, 10 or 12 pairs of tongs, heading tools, punches, six hammers, and one sledge.[25]

The arrangement did not last long. By the next year Nathaniel and Melinda transferred the property to Dow.[26] Nathaniel wanted to occupy part of the house until April 1, 1853, and claim ownership of the crops in the garden. Here was yet another example of Nathaniel's inability to make a go at blacksmithing.

With that 1852 property listing, Nathaniel Brown disappears from the official record. By 1860, his family has been broken up. Melinda is living with the Dow family in Bristol, Vermont, and listed as a servant in the census. Theodore is also part of the Dow family, and noted as Theodore Dow. Samantha and Isidore are residents of the Poor Farm in Williston, under the heading "pauper." Isidore is listed as idiotic; she died on September 2 or 3, 1860. Sarah is apparently living in a rooming house in Colchester, Vermont, and working in one of the mills powered by the falls on the Winooski River. Lucy is living with the George Chapman family in Jericho, Vermont. This is the same family that established the Chapman line in North Williston. Oscar is with the Bishop family in Jericho. The wealth of the Chapman family ($25,000) and of the Bishop family ($22,500) is striking. This indicates that affluent families in the area took in two of the children of Nathaniel and Melinda, one of the ways that communities looked out for the needs of the less fortunate.[27]

On December 29, 1861, Nathaniel and Melinda's daughter Samantha Brown died and was buried in Williston.[28] Why was Samantha at the Poor Farm? Was she ill or disabled and unable to work? She was 24 years old and should have been able to support herself. It is possible she was appointed guardian for Isidore. Melinda died in Richmond at age 49 years, 7 months, 5 days, on December 14, 1865. On May 18, 1870, son Oscar died at age 26 years, 26 days, in Jericho. He was a carpenter.[29]

Had Nathaniel taken off due to the economic pressure of supporting his family, perhaps to California? Had he died? A death record for him could not be located. The final whereabouts of Nathaniel is a mystery.

Sidney H. Wells, in jail with Nathaniel for the grocery store break-in in Akron, settled down in Battle Creek, Michigan, with his wife Mary and family. He died in Kalamazoo in 1886.[30]

What does Reed Brown's journal leave for us? The recounting of his journey gives readers a first-person narrative of the pleasures and challenges of traveling in antebellum America. Reed employed all the modes of transportation available at the time and his descriptions provide us with a greater appreciation of our ability to cross the country rapidly in relative comfort today. At the same time, such high-speed travel may have us wishing for a slower pace to take in the sights with as much interest and curiosity as Reed did. Some things that he experienced have not changed for the traveler over the years: avoiding exhaustion by getting a quiet night's rest in a comfortable establishment, making connections, enjoying, or at least tolerating one's fellow passengers, and the goal of any trip, a safe and satisfactory ending.

Although written in a simple, unsophisticated fashion, the journal also reveals some of Reed's personality traits, interests, and values. Reed was a devout Universalist Christian. He attended church services, frequently remarking on the high quality of sermons, and about the impressive church in Akron. He kept the Sabbath while traveling as best he could and Sunday was the anchor of his week. He did not approve of the consumption of alcohol. He remarked that he was happy to stay in a temperance house because there was less profane language and the guests were quieter.

Reed was very careful with his money, as he kept track of just about every penny spent. The items he observed in the Patent Office Building museum are noted with their monetary value. The ledger portions of his journal show a careful record of business done as a blacksmith, with amounts owed by his customers.

You can take the farmer out of the country, but you can't take the farmer out of the man. Reed constantly recorded the appearance of the crops, the animals, the quality of the soil, and the farming techniques he observed along the way.

Reed did not let the business portion of the trip negate the joys of being a tourist. On the Champlain Canal, he recounted some Revolutionary War history; in New York City, he marveled about the ships in the harbor and the variety of goods in the markets. In Washington, D.C., he took in the Capitol, the president's house, and the Patent Office Building museum. He knew how to have fun and further his own enlightenment by going beyond the tasks of his trip.

Reed was a family man, as most obviously shown in his devotion to freeing his brother Nathaniel from jail, walking many miles to see him although his feet were sore, and asking the guard to let him stay in the cell with him. Reed went to Cleveland to collect exculpatory testimony for his brother. He sat with him for hours in the cell as they awaited the trial, and then again during the trial. He safely escorted Nathaniel and Melinda's family back to Vermont. Reed was committed to his Vermont family as well, writing home and sending them newspapers from time to time.

Reed had a great loyalty to Vermont and Vermonters. He was introduced to them in Ohio, displayed bonds with other Vermonters, and was pleased when he met someone from his home state on his travels.

Reed's persistence and physical stamina were remarkable. He failed to let transportation mishaps, illnesses, or bureaucratic delays deter him from his goals of getting a patent and freeing his brother. Another man might have stopped when his steamboat exploded, but not Reed. He was a man on a mission. And once he got that patent he was going to profit from it, through barter or currency — it didn't matter, if he had something to show for his work.

He went out of his way to help others too; he hand-delivered a letter to Esquire Howard's brother in Buffalo and stopped to help a sick stranger driving a yoke of oxen who was too weak to continue.

Reed's exposure to people of other ethnic groups added to his appreciation of the country. His perceptions about African Americans was widened when he saw them in Washington enjoying themselves on the street. He was also intrigued by the farming and marketing practices of the "Dutch."

Reed's experience with securing a patent for his improved carriage springs provides us with a personal account of the process that was so important to the growth of America's economy in the 19th century. The idea of protecting inventors' rights predates the United States Constitution, where it was encoded into our laws, but the openness and democratization in our country's patent procedures were unique. These characteristics gave the common man, like Reed, not just the trained technicians, a chance to receive his appropriate due after conceiving of a product worthy of patent protection.

Finally, we can speculate on the impact the trip might have had on Reed. He undoubtedly returned to Vermont with a broader view of his country, his fellow citizens, and the physical features of the landscape. The urban areas he visited opened a whole new perspective for him. The conversations he had with Vermonters who had migrated out of state provided viewpoints on the pros and cons of leaving one's home. He experienced some of the trials of urban and westward migration without all the pitfalls of a permanent move. Given all the places he visited, he might have been tempted to consider moving to another part of the country, but he stayed put in Vermont with a new gratefulness for his home. It was an eye-opening, 57-day educational experience.

Reed knew he was on an unusual adventure and that a chronicle of his journey was worth recording. His descendants were probably entertained for years by reading the journal and asking him to tell some stories one more time. The fact that the narrative was passed on in the family for close to 150 years bears witness to the importance of Reed's journey and its historical value to the Browns. That was evident, as well, when Lorraine Brown gave the journal to the Williston Historical Society in 1982.

ℐCKNOWLEDGEMENTS

Many people helped with bringing the Reed Brown journal to publication.

I am especially indebted to the readers of the chapters who provided editorial comments and judgement on historical accuracy. Jane Gramlich, Librarian, Special Collections Akron-Summit County Public Library, aided with the early research and read the Ohio chapters; Anne Rollins and Jessica Smith of the Historical Society of Washington, D.C.; Peter James, Abbot-Downing Historical Society (NH); Mariam Touba, Reference Librarian, Patricia D. Klingenstein Library of The New-York Historical Society; Eloise Beil, Senior Editor, Lake Champlain Maritime Museum, Vergennes, VT; and Sarah Kozma, Oneida County (NY) Historical Association. Alan Berolzheimer did the overall editing and brought the story all together with his superior professional skills.

These people helped with research and supported the project: Weckea Lily, Pennsylvania Historical Society; John Ball, University of Akron; Elizabeth Barton, Educational Specialist, United States Botanic Garden; David Beebe, Camillus, NY historian; Dr. Russell P. Bellico, maritime historian; Robert Belvin, New Brunswick (NJ) Free Public Library; Jane Bennett, Building Stone Institute; Cathleen Brennan, National Archives and Records Administration; Marlo Broad, Alpena County (MI) Library; Frank Brusca, independent historian; Sarah Buffington, Curator, Old Economy Village, Ambridge, PA; Prudence Doherty and Christopher Burns, Special Collections, University of Vermont.

Also Suzanna Calev, Reference Librarian, New-York Historical Society; Debra Callahan, independent genealogist; Devin Colman, Vermont State Architectural Historian; Marcus Cook, Visitor Services Division, U.S. Capitol; Bruce Cridlebaugh, Pittsburgh bridge expert; Davideen DeGraff, Brown family descendant; Mariessa Dobrick, Vermont State Archives and Records Administration; Tim Duerden, Delaware County (NY) Historical Association; Anita Dulak, Little Falls (NY) Historical Society; Kristi Finefield, Reference Librarian, Prints and Photographs Division, Library of Congress.

Marie Gandron, Skenesborough Museum, Whitehall, NY; Francesca Giannetti, Digital Humanities Librarian, Archibald S. Alexander Library, Rutgers, The State University of New Jersey; Kevin Gray, Reference Librarian, Reed Memorial Library, Ravenna, OH.

Patricia Poore, Judy Hayward and Peter Miller of Aimmedia; Leianne Heppner, President and CEO Summit County (OH) Historical Society; Linda Kaiser, Archivist, Waterbury (VT) Historical Society; Judy Kaplan, retired librarian; Jerry Kelly, Baltimore Street Car Museum; Randy Kirschner, wheelwright, Charlie Lake, British Columbia.

Emily Koetsier, Billings Farm and Museum, Woodstock, VT; Allynne Lange, Hudson River Maritime Museum, Kingston, NY; Peter Liebhold, National Museum of American History; Ashley Maready, Curator, Erie Canal Museum, Syracuse, NY.

Rick and Robin MacRae, of Paterson, NY; Andrew Mayer, Ohio History Connection; Robert Moore, historian at the Great Arch in St. Louis; Robert Murtagh, National Customs Museum Foundation; Paul Nelson, Cleveland fire historian; Dr. Robert Nielsen, Professor of Agronomy, Purdue University; Trish Norman, Farmers' Museum, Cooperstown, NY.

Francis P. O'Neill, Maryland Historical Society; David Perdue, Charles Dickens webpage; Stephen Perkins, Executive Director of the Vermont Historical Society; Ronald Petrie, Canal Society of Ohio; Richard Pletcher, Amish Acres, Nappanee, IN.

Gerald and Marianne Riordan of North Williston, VT. Ruth Setterquist, Solano County (CA) Genealogical Society; Carol Sheriff, author of *The Artificial River;* Carter Smith, Champlain Valley School District (VT); Dr. D. Phillip Sponenberg, Professor, Pathology and Genetics, Virginia-Maryland College of Veterinary Medicine; Paul Carnahan and Marjorie Strong, Vermont Historical Society; Richard Taylor, University of Delaware; Charles Tinker, Fletcher, VT historian.

Sean Trainor, historian, Gainesville, FL; Cynthia Van Ness, The Buffalo History Museum; Amanda Vaughan, Maumee (OH) Valley Historical Society; George N. Vourlojianis, John Carroll University; Ramona Walker, Portage County (OH) Records Center; Mike Walzer and Matt Bland, Mustill Store Museum, Akron; Craig Williams, New York State Canal Society.

A special thank you to Paul Wood, farm implement and patent expert, author, presenter, and supporter, for sharing his encyclopedic knowledge of the 19th century.

The Williston Historical Society board provided permission to reproduce the journal, and financial support: Terence Macaig, past president, Brenda Perkins, current president, Robert Bradish, Marlene Price, Stephen Perkins, Adrienne Katz, Jon Stokes, and Meghan Cope.

Daughters Jill and Elizabeth helped with the transcribing, editing, and indexing. My wife, Lucille, was always very supportive and enjoyed the research trips along the Champlain and Erie Canals, to Akron, New York City, Washington, D.C. and numerous small towns and museums in Vermont and New York.

Credit must be given to Sue Storey for the book design and layout, and Rachel Fisher of Onion River Press for guidance with the publishing. I owe an enormous debt of gratitude to all these people.

*N*OTES

INTRODUCTION

1. Reed and Electa Brown's fifth child was Byron Briggs Brown, who was the father of Lewis D. Brown, Lorraine Brown's father.

2. Charles Dickens, *American Notes* (1842; London: Penguin Books, 2004), xi.

3. Mark Walston, "Exploring the American Experience," *Domestic Manners of the Americans*. October 21, 2015, https://markwalston.com/2015/10/21/domestic-manners-of-the-americans/ (accessed May 31, 2017).

CHAPTER 1

1. Michael Sherman, Gene Sessions, and P. Jeffrey Potash, *Freedom and Unity: A History of Vermont* (Barre: Vermont Historical Society, 2004), 195

2. *Burlington Weekly Free Press* (Burlington, VT), 27 March 1868.

3. Ogden J. Ross, *The Steamboats of Lake Champlain, 1809-1930* (Rutland, VT: Vermont Heritage Press, 1997), 66.

4. Ralph Nading Hill, *Lake Champlain: Key to Liberty* (Montpelier, VT: Vermont Life Magazine, 1976), 199-200.

5. The author is indebted to historian and author Russell P. Bellico for providing the background information for this possible explanation. E-mail message to the author, June 19, 2017.

6. Charles Dickens, *American Notes* (1842; London: Penguin Books, 2004), 233-234.

7. Ibid., 234.

8. *Burlington Free Press*, 18 November 1836.

9. J. C. Furnas, *The Americans: A Social History of the United States, 1587-1914* (New York: G.P. Putnam's Sons, 1969), 128-129.

10. *Green-Mountain Freeman* (Montpelier, VT), 7 September 1848.

11. Skenesborough Museum, Whitehall, New York display, accessed August 12, 2016. Peter Comstock (1798-1874) was an entrepreneur who helped develop transportation in the Champlain Valley with "rafting…stage coach lines, a ferry boat line, and large lake boats." Rose Kana, "County Historical Group Hears Peter Comstock Story," *Post-Star* (Glen Falls, NY), 5 October 1974.

12. Russell P. Bellico, *Sails and Steam in the Mountains: A Maritime and Military History of Lake George and Lake Champlain* (Fleischmanns, NY: Purple Mountain Press, 1992), 239, 244.

13. Hill, *Lake Champlain*, 207.

14. Lakes to Locks Passage: New York's Great Northeast Journey, "The Canal Era: The Champlain Canal and the Growth of America," https://www.lakestolocks.org/content/entry/ltlF3922AFFB3B8F90C9 (accessed May 14, 2017).

15. The spelling of Fort Ann/Anne varied through the ages depending upon the occupying force and namesake. Today the town is Fort Ann.

16. *Green-Mountain Freeman*, 7 September 1848.

17. "The question of where to locate the eastern terminal of the Erie Canal provoked great controversy between the cities of Albany and Troy. The route which was finally selected went from Schenectady to Cohoes and then south along the west bank of the Hudson River to Albany. This plan to have the last stretch of the canal terminate in Albany and thus by-pass the city of Troy absolutely infuriated the Troy business community. In order to provide equally convenient access to the Erie Canal for Troy commerce and west-bound freight that did not need to stop at the Port of Albany, a short lateral canal was constructed to connect the City of West Troy (now Watervliet) with the tide waters of the Hudson River. This short cut (Side Cut) to the Erie Canal ran about where present day 23rd Street is." HMdb.org, The Historical Marker Database, "Watervliet in Albany County, New York—The American Northeast (Mid-Atlantic), Erie Canal," http://www.hmdb.org/marker.asp?MarkerID=12214 (accessed May 14, 2017).

18. Albany Institute of History & Art, "Albany from the East Side of the River," http://www.albanyinstitute.org/details/items/albany-from-the-east-side-of-the-river.html (accessed May 26, 2018).

19. Information is from George W. Murdock, a steam engineer who worked on the Hudson River boats in his younger days. The write-ups were published in the Kingston (New York) *Daily Freeman* in the 1930s. Provided by Allynne Lange, curator, Hudson River Maritime Museum, Kingston, New York.

20. James F. Leiner, "Steamboats on the Hudson River," *The Rockland Post*, 1 September 2016, http://www.rocklandpost.com/2016/09/01/steamboats-on-the-hudson-river/ (accessed December 6, 2016). See also Clifford Browder, "No Place for Normal: New York, Steamboat Wars on the Hudson," http://cbrowder.blogspot.com/2013/04/58-steamboat-wars-on-hudson.html, April 28, 2013 (accessed December 7, 2016).

21. "Accident on the River," *New York Tribune*, 25 September 1841.

22. *New York Tribune*, 26 March 1842.

CHAPTER 2

1. *Morning Herald* (New York, NY), 24 September 1840.

2. *Sheldon & Co.'s Business or Advertising Directory: Containing the Cards, Circulars, and Advertisements of the Principal Firms of the Cities of New-York, Boston, Philadelphia, Baltimore, Etc., Etc.* (New York: John F. Trow & Company, 1845), 3-8.

3. Edwin G. Burrows and Mike Wallace, *Gotham: A History of New York City to 1898* (New York: Oxford University Press, 1999), 532.

4. "Introduction to Temperance Reform for Teachers," http://www.teachushistory.org/Temperance/forteachers.htm (accessed October 31, 2016).

5. "New York Custom House Records," New York Public Library, Archives and Manuscripts, http://archives.nypl.org/mss/3092 (accessed November 5, 2016).

6. William Elliot, *The Washington Guide* (Washington, D.C.: Frank Taylor, 1837), 230-238.

7. Thomas P. Jones, ed., *Journal of the Franklin Institute of the State of Pennsylvania and Mechanics Register Devoted to Mechanical and Physical Science, Civil Engineering, the Arts, and Manufactures, and the Recording of American and Other Patented Inventions* (Philadelphia: Franklin Institute, 1836), 27: 129.

8. Kenneth W. Dobyns, *The Patent Office Pony: A History of the Early Patent Office* (Fredericksburg, VA: Sergeant Kirkland's Museum and Historical Society, 1994), 96-97.

9. Ibid., 97.

10. Burrows and Wallace, *Gotham*, 564-565.

11. Charles Dickens, *American Notes* (1842; London: Penguin Books, 2004), 93.

12. Reed's grandfather, John Brown, born May 7, 1758, had married Mary Grow on June 20, 1779. She was born September 7, 1753. Reed's father, John Brown Jr., married Betsy Grow of Tunbridge, Vermont, after his first wife, Reed's mother, died. Unless otherwise noted, genealogy and census information throughout this text was taken from Ancestry.com, supplemented by town, state, and national records where necessary.

13. *Klondike Sun* (Dawson City, Canada), 17 April 2013. "Wales F. Grow began his career with the co-operative 'New York Pianoforte Manufacturing Company' and is listed as a partner in 'A. H. Gale & Company' in 1842. In 1847, Grow left the partnership with A. H. Gale to join William Christopher, establishing the firm of 'Grow & Christopher.' The firm specialized in square grand pianos, and by 1855 Grow & Christopher was building over 150 pianos annually. Instruments by Grow & Christopher were frequently exhibited at fairs and trade shows and were generally awarded with high honors for design and construction. Grow & Christopher dissolved around 1857-1858, and there is no mention of either Grow or Christopher being active in the piano industry after about 1860." See also Nancy Groce, *Musical Instrument Makers of New York: A Directory of Eighteenth and Nineteenth Century Urban Craftsmen* (Stuyvesant, NY: Pendragon Press, 1991), 66-67.

14. Asa Greene, *A Glance at New York Embracing the City Government, Theatres, Hotels, Churches, Mobs, Monopolies, Learned Professions, Newspapers, Rogues, Dandies, Fires and Firemen, Water and Other Liquids* (New York: Asa Greene, 1837), 253-254.

15. Ibid., 142. See also pages 124-142 for a complete description of the newspapers in New York City in 1837.

16. Ibid., 4.

17. Dickens, *American Notes*, 90-108. The Five Points neighborhood of New York City was infamous for crime, prostitution, and disease. It was the subject of Martin Scorsese's movie, *The Gangs of New York* (2002). For a detailed description see Tyler Anbinder, *Five Points: The 19th-Century New York City Neighborhood That Invented Tap Dance, Stole Elections,*

and Became the World's Most Notorious Slum (New York: The Free Press, 2001).

18. Daniel W. Howe, *What Hath God Wrought: The Transformation of America, 1815-1848* (New York: Oxford University Press, 2007), 217.

19. Greene, *A Glance at New York*, 214-215.

20. Dickens, *American Notes*, 89.

21. Edward Ruggles, *A Picture of New-York in 1846; with a Short Account of Places in its Vicinity; Designed as a Guide to Citizens and Strangers* (New York: Homans and Ellis, 1846), 87-90.

22. Quoted in Patra Jongjitirat, "How Markets Grow: Learning from Manhattan's Lost Food Hub," November 25, 2012, Project for Public Spaces, http://www.pps.org/blog/how-markets-grow-learning-from-manhattans-lost-food-hub/ (accessed November 5, 2016).

23. American Kennel Club, http://www.akc.org/dog-breeds/maltesc/ (accessed December 12, 2016).

CHAPTER 3

1. Federal Writers' Project of the Works Progress Administration for the State of New Jersey, *New Jersey: A Guide to its Present and Past* (New York: Hastings House, 1939), 101.

2. Francis P. O'Neill, reference librarian, Maryland Historical Society, e-mail message to author, November 16, 2016.

3. *New Brunswick, Its History, Its Homes, Its Industries. The New Brunswick Times* (New Brunswick, NJ: The Times Publishing Company, 1908), 28-29, 34-35. See also "Town Thrives as Crossroad Between New York, Pennsylvania," City-data.com., http://www.city-data.com/us-cities/The-Northeast/New-Brunswick-History.html (accessed January 14, 2017).

4. Mark Aldrich, *Death Rode the Rails: American Railroad Accidents and Safety, 1828-1965* (Baltimore: Johns Hopkins University Press, 2006), 38.

5. Ibid., 10-41.

6. Robert C. Reed, *Train Wrecks: A Pictorial History of Accidents on The Main Line* (Seattle: Superior Publishing Company, 1968), 9.

7. *Polynesian* (Honolulu), 6 June 1840.

8. *Morning Herald* (New York), 26 November 1840.

9. Charles Dickens, *American Notes* (1842; London: Penguin Books, 2004), 72-75.

10. John Hepp, "Omnibuses," *The Encyclopedia of Greater Philadelphia*, http://philadelphiaencyclopedia.org/archive/omnibuses/ (accessed November 8, 2016); see also Edwin G. Burrows and Mike Wallace, *Gotham: A History of New York City to 1898* (New York: Oxford University Press, 1999), 565.

11. Dr. Robert L. Nielsen, e-mail message to author, August 8, 2016.

12. Burrows and Wallace, *Gotham*, 565.

13. John Hepp, "Railroads," *Encyclopedia of Greater Philadelphia*, http://philadelphiaencyclopedia.org/archive/railroads/ (accessed December 13, 2016).

14. Francis P. O'Neill, Maryland Historical Society, e-mail message to author, November 16, 2016. "Originally [circa 1829] the Baltimore & Ohio Railroad, which ran south from here to Washington and west to Wheeling, West Virginia, had its Baltimore terminus first at Mount Clare in far west Baltimore, and later at Camden Yards, just west of Charles Street. The Baltimore & Susquehanna Railroad, which ran north from Baltimore to Harrisburg, Pennsylvania, had its station first at the 'Bolton Lot' in (for its time) far north Baltimore, and later at Calvert Street, north of Baltimore Street. The Philadelphia, Wilmington & Baltimore Railroad, which connected us with Philadelphia and Wilmington as of the 1840s, built its Baltimore depot at President Street, which was both south of Baltimore Street and east of Charles Street. Nobody's trains could get to anybody else's station except via a ribbon of track which the city of Baltimore laid out along Pratt Street to connect President Street and Camden Stations. The city fathers, however, were opposed to 'the cars' actually steaming through the business district, so they stipulated that both passengers and freight had to be dragged from one station to the other by the teams [Reed] …described and could only be coupled back on to a locomotive when they were once again on railroad property."

15. Daniel W. Howe, *What Hath God Wrought: The Transformation of America, 1815-1848* (New York: Oxford University Press, 2007), 501-508; see also Burrows and Wallace, *Gotham*, 611-625.

16. Dickens, *American Notes*, 110.

17. Elise A. Guyette, *Discovering Black Vermont: African American Farmers in Hinesburgh, 1790-1890* (Lebanon, NH: University Press of New England, 2010), 22.

18. Dickens, *American Notes*, 127.

19. Francis M. Trollope, *Domestic Manners of the Americans* (London: Whittaker, Treacher, & Co., 1832), 180.

CHAPTER 4

1. *The Washingtonian*, 23 August 1845.

2. Matthew B. Gilmore, "District of Columbia Population History," Washington, D.C. History Resources, https://matthewbgilmore.wordpress.com/district-of-columbia-population-history/ (accessed November 11, 2016). Population figures are for the District of Columbia and do include Alexandria City/County up until the 1846 retrocession back to Virginia.

3. Tom Lewis, *Washington: A History of Our National City* (New York: Basic Books, 2015), 126-139.

4. Population of the 100 Largest Urban Places: 1840. U.S. Bureau of the Census, Internet Release date: June 15, 1998. https://www.census.gov/population/www/documentation/twps0027/tab07.txt (accessed November 16, 2016). Leslie M. Harris, "African-Americans in New York City, 1626-1863," Emory University Department of History Newsletter, No. 46, August 2001, http://history.emory.edu/newsletter01/

newsl01/african.htm (accessed November 16, 2016).

5. Dody W. Smith, "Our Oldest Naval Memorial: The Tripoli Monument," Naval History Blog, https://www.navalhistory.org/2011/05/30/the-tripoli-monument (accessed November 17, 2016).

6. "The Old Patent Office Building, the City's First National Museum," Streets of Washington: Stories and Images of Historic Washington, D.C., http://www.streetsofwashington.com/2015/05/the-old-patent-office-building-citys.html (accessed October 17, 2017). See also Charles J. Robertson, *Temple of Invention: History of a National Landmark*, (New York: Scala Arts Publishers, Inc., 2006).

7. "General Post Office, Washington, D.C." General Services Administration, https://www.gsa.gov/historic-buildings/general-post-office-washington-dc#overview (accessed October 17, 2017).

8. Henry L. Ellsworth, *A Digest of Patents Issued by the United States, Including the Years 1839, 1840, 1841* (Washington, D.C.: Printed by William Greer, 1842), 59.

9. Francis M. Trollope, *Domestic Manners of the Americans* (London: Whittaker, Treacher, & Co., 1832), 178.

10. Paul Wood, e-mail message to author, April 15, 2016.

11. Randy Kirschner, e-mail message to author, April 13, 2016.

12. Paul Wood, e-mail message to author, April 2, 2017.

13. Daniel W. Howe, *What Hath God Wrought: The Transformation of America, 1815-1848* (New York: Oxford University Press, 2007), 534-535. See also Kenneth Sokoloff and Zorina Kahn, "The Democratization of Invention," *Journal of Economic History* 59 (1990): 363-378. B. Zorina Khan, "An Economic History of Patent Institutions," https://eh.net/encyclopedia/an-economic-history-of-patent-institutions/ (accessed August 15, 2017); B. Zorina Khan, *The Democratization of Invention: Patents and Copyrights in American Economic Development* (New York: Cambridge University Press, 2005); B. Zorina Khan "Innovations in Intellectual Property Systems and Economic Development" http://economics.yale.edu/sites/default/files/files/Workshops-Seminars/Economic-History/khan-020328.pdf (accessed August 16, 2017).

14. Webster's Dictionary 1828, Online Edition, American Dictionary of the English Language http://webstersdictionary1828.com.

15. Nathaniel Philbrick, "The Scientific Legacy of the U.S. Exploring Expedition," http://www.sil.si.edu/DigitalCollections/usexex/learn/Philbrick.htm (accessed June 1, 2017). For a complete description of the expedition, see Nathaniel Philbrick, *Sea of Glory: America's Voyage of Discovery: The U.S. Exploring Expedition, 1838-1842* (New York: Penguin Group, 2003).

16. "A Most Unusual Bequest," Smithsonian Mobile, http://m.si.edu/#highlightDetail/15/highlightId=649 (accessed June 4, 2017). See also Herman J. Viola and Carolyn Margolis, eds. *Magnificent Voyagers: The U. S. Exploring Expedition, 1838-1842*, (Washington D.C.: Smithsonian Institution Press, 1985), 229-230; Dr. Jane Walsh, "Learn

More About the U.S. Exploring Expedition, From the Ends of the Earth, The United States Exploring Expedition Collections," http://www.sil.si.edu/DigitalCollections/usexex/learn.htm.

17. *Domestic Letters, 1784-1906*, Department of State (RG 59): https://catalog.archives.gov/id/29730448 (accessed July 6, 2016).

18. Alfred Hunter, *A Popular Catalogue of the Extraordinary Curiosities in the National Institute Arranged in the Building Belonging to the Patent Office*, https://catalog.hathitrust.org/Record/008602690, (accessed April 19, 2017).

19. De B. R. Keim, *Keim's Illustrated Guide to the Museum of Models, Patent Office* (Washington D.C.: De B. R. Keim, 1874), https://lccn.loc.gov/05024969 (accessed April 20, 2017).

20. Keim, *Guide*, 12.

21. Trollope, *Domestic Manners*, 179.

22. Hunter, *A Popular Catalogue*, 37.

23. Ibid., 33.

24. Ibid., 48-49.

25. Ibid., 49.

26. Dickens, *American Notes*, 137.

27. Ibid., 138.

28. Carol R. Joynt and Hallie Golden, "White House Security Updates in the Past Century: A Timeline," *Washingtonian*, September 22, 2014, https://www.washingtonian.com/2014/09/22/white-house-security-updates-in-the-past-century/ (accessed November 29, 2016).

29. "The Evolution of White House Security," November 17, 2014, *The Tenley Times*, https://tenleytimes.wordpress.com/2014/11/17/the-evolution-of-white-house-security/ (accessed November 29, 2016).

30. Simon Schama, *The American Future: A History* (New York: HarperCollins Publishers, 2009), 63-64.

31. Dickens, *American Notes*, 129-130.

CHAPTER 5

1. "Thomas Viaduct & Relay, Maryland Railroad History," http://thomas-viaduct-relay-maryland.blogspot.com/2014/06/the-viaduct-hotel-train-station-in-relay_2423.html (accessed December 26, 2016).

2. Information provided by Weckea Lilly, researcher at the Historical Society of Pennsylvania. Several alternative side routes were also suggested.

3. D. Phillip Sponenberg, DVM, Ph.D., Professor, Pathology and Genetics, Virgin-

ia-Maryland College of Veterinary Medicine, Virginia Tech, Blacksburg, Virginia, e-mail message to author, May 23, 2017.

4. J. Percy Hart, *Hart's History and Directory of the Three Towns, Brownsville, Bridgeport, West Brownsville, Also Abridged History of Fayette County & Western Pennsylvania* (Cadwallader, PA: J. P. Hart, 1904), 74.

5. John N. Boucher and John W. Jordan, eds., *History of Westmoreland County, Pennsylvania* (New York: Lewis Publishing Company, 1906), 254-255 https://archive.org/stream/ historyofwestmor01bouc#page/254/mode/2up (accessed December 23, 2016). See also Leah Binkovitz, *Going West: The American History Museum's Conestoga Wagon is a Must-See*, November 14, 2012, http://www.smithsonianmag.com/smithsonian-institution/ going-west-the-american-history-museums-conestoga-wagon-is-a-must-see-121785645/ (accessed December 20, 2016); "Conestoga Wagon," http://www.history.com/topics/ conestoga-wagon History.com, 2010 (accessed December 22, 2016).

6. "How New Hampshire's Lewis Downing Conquered the West." New England Historical Society, http://www.newenglandhistoricalsociety.com/new-hampshires-lewis-downing-conquered-west (accessed December 22, 2016). See also Abbott-Downing Historical Society. http://concordcoach.org/index.html (accessed December 22, 2016); "The Concord Coach," Concord (NH) Historical Society, http://www.concordhistoricalsociety.org/the-concord-coach (accessed December 22, 2016); Mary A. Helmich, *Stage Styles — Not All Were Coaches!* Interpretation & Education Division, California State Parks, 2008, http:// www.parks.ca.gov/?page_id=25449 (accessed December 22, 2016).

7. Charles Dickens, *American Notes* (1842; London: Penguin Books, 2004), 147-150.

8. Ibid., 156-158.

9. Paul Wood, e-mail message to author, December 8, 2016.

10. J. C. Furnas, *The Americans: A Social History of the United States, 1587-1914* (New York: G.P. Putnam's Sons, 1969), 86-87. See also, Penn Historical and Museum Commission, *Pennsylvania Architectural Field Guide, Barns and Outbuildings, 1700-1930*, http://www.phmc. state.pa.us/portal/communities/architecture/styles/barns-outbuildings.html (accessed August 6, 2017).

11. Philip Nicklin, *Journey Through Pennsylvania — 1835: By Canal, Rail and Stage Coach* (originally titled *A Pleasant Peregrination Through the Prettiest Parts of Pennsylvania, Performed by Peregrine Prolix*) (Philadelphia: Grigg and Elliot, 1836), 37-38.

12. Nathaniel Hawthorne, *The Complete Works of Nathaniel Hawthorne*, Volume 9. George P. Lathrop and Julian Hawthorne, eds. (Boston: Houghton-Mifflin, 1883), 184.

13. Albert C. Rose, *Historic American Roads: From Frontier Trails to Superhighways* (New York: Crown Publishers, Inc., 1976), 36.

14. Daniel W. Howe, *What Hath God Wrought: The Transformation of America, 1815-1848* (New York: Oxford University Press, 2007), 213-214.

15. Essex, Vermont, Land Records, Volume 7, 158.

16. Dickens, *American Notes*, 172-173.

17. Nicklin, *Journey*, 57-59.

18. "Yankee," Wikipedia, https://en.wikipedia.org/wiki/Yankee, (accessed May 27, 2018).

19. Furnas, *The Americans*, 245.

20. James D. McNiven, "Yankee Peddlers," http://theyankeeroad.com/index.php/yankee-peddlers (accessed January 4, 2017). See also Furnas, *The Americans*, 244-247.

21. Frances M. Trollope, *Domestic Manners of the Americans* (London: Whittaker, Treacher, & Co., 1832), 294-295.

22. George W. Knepper, *Ohio and Its People* (Kent, OH: Kent State University Press, 2003), 141-142.

23. Dickens, *American Notes*, 176-177.

24. Sean Patrick Adams, "The US Coal Industry in the Nineteenth Century," https://eh.net/encyclopedia/the-us-coal-industry-in-the-nineteenth-century-2/ (accessed January 5, 2017). See also Susan J. Tewalt, et. al., "A Digital Resource Model of the Upper Pennsylvania Pittsburgh Coal Bed, Monongahela Group, Northern Appalachian Basin Coal Region," https://pubs.usgs.gov/pp/p1625c/CHAPTER_C/CHAPTER_C.pdf (accessed January 5, 2017).

25. Isaac Harris, *Harris' General Business Directory of the Cities of Pittsburgh and Allegheny: and also of the Most Flourishing and Important Towns and Cities of Pennsylvania, Ohio, Western New York, Virginia, &c.* (Pittsburgh: A.A. Anderson, 1841), 232-235, https://archive.org/stream/harrisgeneralbus_01harr#page/n5/mode/2up (accessed April 9, 2018).

26. "America and the Utopian Dream," http://brbl-archive.library.yale.edu/exhibitions/utopia/uc05.html (accessed January 7, 2017). See also "Third Home of the Harmony Society," Old Economy Village, http://oldeconomyvillage.org/ (accessed January 7, 2017). Sarah Buffington, curator, Old Economy Village, e-mail message to author, May 31, 2016.

CHAPTER 6

1. Becky Odom, curator, Ohio History Connection, quoted in e-mail message from Andrew Mayer to author, January 17, 2017.

2. *Weekly Graphic* (Kirksville, MO), 27 July 1888.

3. *The Pilot and Transcript* (Baltimore), 31 October 1840.

4. Henry Howe, *Historical Collections of Ohio in Two Volumes, an Encyclopedia of the State*, (Columbus, OH: Henry Howe and Son, 1888), 1: 203-204.

5. Steven Seidman, "The Log Cabin Campaign: Image Deception in 1840," http://www.ithaca.edu/rhp/programs/cmd/blogs/posters_and_election_propaganda/the_log_cabin_campaign:_image_deception_in_1840/ (accessed January 11, 2017).

6. Michael Sherman, Gene Sessions, and P. Jeffery Potash, *Freedom and Unity: A History of Vermont* (Barre: Vermont Historical Society, 2004), 198.

7. *Burlington Free Press*, 17 July 1840.

8. *Portage County Democrat* (Ravenna, OH), 17 December 1873.

9. *Portage Sentinel* (Ravenna, OH), 26 November 1845.

10. *Green-Mountain Freeman* (Montpelier, VT), 14 September 1848.

11. Charles Dickens, *American Notes* (1842; London: Penguin Books, 2004), 208-209.

12. *The United States District Court for the District of Vermont, Bankruptcy Act of 1841 Case Files, Case No. 997, Nathaniel Brown*. National Archives and Records Administration, 400 West Pershing Road, Kansas City, Missouri 64108.

13. Thomas G. Gregory, Christina M. McVay, and Dennis R. Sutton. *Ravenna: A Bicentennial Album of Nineteenth-Century Photographs* (Ravenna, OH: Portage County Historical Society, 1999), 54.

14. Samuel A. Lane, *Fifty Years and Over of Akron and Summit County* (Akron, OH: Beacon Job Department, 1892), 101-102.

15. Ibid., 551.

16. Karl H. Grismer, *Akron and Summit County* (Akron, OH: Summit County Historical Society, 1952), 119. For an overall view of the Ohio & Erie Canal see George W. Knepper, *Ohio and Its People* (Kent, OH: Kent State University Press, 2003), 144-153.

17. Oscar E. Olin, *Akron and Environs: Historical, Biographical, Genealogical* (Chicago and New York: The Lewis Publishing Company, 1917), 135, 137.

18. Lane, *Fifty Years*, 447.

19. The Canal Society of Ohio has a transcription of *The Boats of the Ohio Canal, 1839-1855*, on its website with this information on the *D. Adams*: "Cleveland Aug 7, 1840. I, Isaac Austin, residing in Chillicothe, Ross County, Ohio do certify that I am the owner of the canal boat *D. Adams of Chillicothe*. Signed Isaac Austin. Collectors Office, Cleveland Aug 7/40. I certify that the foregoing are correct copies of the certificates of registry for the boats *Sousanne, B. F. Conway, and D. Adams* now on file and recorded in this office." http://www.canalsocietyohio.org/cso-documents.html, 31 (accessed January 20, 2017).

20. The author is indebted to Paul Nelson of the Cleveland Fire Museum and Fire Historian for this information. E-mail message to author, August 31, 2016.

21. Peter L. Bernstein, *Wedding of the Waters: The Erie Canal and the Making of a Great Nation* (New York: W. W. Norton and Company, 2005), 328.

22. Lane, *Fifty Years*, 36.

23. *Summit County Beacon* (Akron, OH), 6 July 1842. Merrick married Adaline Wells of Williston, Vermont (1812-1902). The 1860 United States census shows they had a daughter, Sonia, 19, a music teacher, and a son, John W., 13, both born in Ohio. Merrick served as a town marshal and constable. The 1870 and 1880 censuses list him as a store clerk. Merrick died on February 3, 1891.

24. Lane, *Fifty Years*, 32.

25. Ibid., 47.

26. Grismer, *Akron and Summit County*, 101-102.

27. William H. Perrin, ed., *History of Summit County with an Outline Sketch of Ohio* (Chicago: Baskin & Battey, 1881), 371-372. See also Lane, *Fifty Years*, 196-198.

28. Daniel W. Howe, *What Hath God Wrought: The Transformation of America, 1815-1848* (New York: Oxford University Press, 2007), 505.

29. Knepper, *Ohio and Its People*, 138-139.

30. Although we do not know Mr. Converse's first name, it is possible he is referring to Elias Smith Converse of Mantua, in neighboring Portage County. Converse was born in Randolph, Vermont, in 1808, married in 1838, and resided in Mantua until his death in 1868. He might have returned to Vermont, but only for a short duration.

31. *Summit County Beacon*, 14 July 1841.

32. With Reed's penchant for gravitating toward fellow Vermonters, Reed could be referring to Calvin and Charlotte Spafford. Calvin was born in Vergennes, Vermont, in 1809.

33. Dr. E. W. Howard was born in Andover, Vermont, on April 14, 1816, the seventh of ten children. He graduated from Berkshire Medical College in Pittsfield, Massachusetts, in 1838. He practiced with his cousin, Professor R. L. Howard in Elyria, Ohio, for a year, and moved to Akron. Perrin, *History of Summit County*, 719.

34. Lane, *Fifty Years*, 1048.

35. William B. Doyle, *Centennial History of Summit County, Ohio and Representative Citizens* (Chicago: Biographical Publishing, 1908), 119. See also Lane, *Fifty Years*, 796.

36. *Pittsburgh Gazette*, 11 August 1840.

37. *Buffalo Whig and Journal*, 18 March 1835.

38. H. N. Walker, *Buffalo City Directory*, 1842 (Buffalo: Steele's Press, 1842), 264.

39. *Summit County Beacon*, 2 March 1842.

40. *Maumee City Express* (OH), 26 January, 7 September 1839.

41. Marian J. Morton, "Temperance," *The Encyclopedia of Cleveland History*, http://ech.case.edu/cgi/article.pl?id=T1 (accessed January 30, 2017).

42. "Cleveland Grays," Ohio History Central, http://www.ohiohistorycentral.org/w/Cleveland_Grays (accessed January 28, 2017). One historian responded to my inquiry on this marching at night. "I checked through my sources and could not find anything specific on why the Grays might be marching at midnight on October 30, 1841. There are references to them turning out at night and firing cannon and musket (for a fee) during William Henry Harrison's election campaign of 1840. There are also refer-

ences to late night "stag dances" at which the members indulged in spirits and tobacco. Nothing specific appears for the night mentioned in the diary. I also checked the
calendar for patriotic events that might be honored by a parade and nothing appears
on October 30." George N. Vourlojianis, Ph.D., Emeritus Professor of History, John
Carroll University, University Heights, Ohio. E-mail message to author, May 6, 2018.

43. *Fort Bragg Advocate* (CA), 11 October 1893.

44. George Whipple obituary, *Geauga Republican* (Bostwick, OH), 7 February 1894.

45. The author is indebted to George Whipple's third great-granddaughter, Debra Callahan, for providing information on her ancestors. E-mail message to author, January 31,
2017.

46. Lewis D. Stilwell, *Migration from Vermont* (Montpelier: Vermont Historical Society, 1948),
171-196.

47. Ibid., 214.

48. Dickens, *American Notes*, 214.

CHAPTER 7

1. *Summit County Beacon*, 23 March 1842. An October 2016 search for the Summit County
court records of the trial revealed that they were probably long discarded.

2. Willis Sibley, "Bridges"; see also "Ohio City," *Encyclopedia of Cleveland History*, Case Western Reserve University, https://case.edu/ech/ (accessed April 4, 2018).

3. Julius P. Bolivar Mac Cabe, *Directory for Cleveland and Ohio City, for the Years 1837-38, Com-
prising Historical and Descriptive Sketches of Each Place* (Cleveland: Sanford & Lot, 1837), 70.

4. Charles Dickens, *American Notes* (1842; London: Penguin Books, 2004), 211.

5. "Minnesota's Lake Superior Shipwrecks, History and Development of Great Lakes
Water Craft," http://www.mnhs.org/places/nationalregister/shipwrecks/mpdf/
mpdf2.php (accessed February 6, 2017). See also "Wisconsin Maritime Museum,
Gerald C. Metzler Great Lakes Vessel Database," http://www.greatlakesvessels.org/
(accessed February 5, 2017); "Passenger and Package Freight Steamers," http://www.
riverboatdaves.com/areas/greatlakes.html (accessed March 28, 2017).

6. Mark Torregrossa, "The Gales of November: What Are They and Why in Michigan?"
2014, www.mlive.com/weather/index.ssf/2014/11/the_gales_of_november_what_are.
html (accessed February 7, 2017). For a description of the 1842 storm see J. B. Mans-
field, ed., *History of the Great Lakes, Volume I*, (Chicago: J. H. Beers & Co., 1899) Chapter
36, 1841-1850, http://www.maritimehistoryofthegreatlakes.ca/documents/hgl/de-
fault.asp?ID=s036 (accessed February 5, 2017).

7. Dickens, *American Notes*, 218-219. Although Dickens does not mention the *Constitution*
by name, it is referred to in Hewson L. Peeke, "Charles Dickens in Ohio in 1842," *Ohio
Archaeological and Historical Quarterly*, 38 (January 1919): 72-81.

CHAPTER 8

1. "The City of Buffalo — 1840 to 1850," Buffalonet: Buffalo's and Western New York's Internet Historical Resource, http://history.buffalonet.org/1840-50.html (accessed February 17, 2017).

2. Frances M. Trollope, *Domestic Manners of the Americans* (London: Whittaker, Treacher, & Co., 1832), 310.

3. Ibid., 306.

4. Thomas X. Grasso, "The Erie Canal's Western Terminus–Commercial Slip, Harbor Development and Canal District," http://buffaloah.com/h/bflo/grasso.pdf, 13 (accessed February 20, 2017).

5. "City of Buffalo 1832 to 1840—The Early Years," Buffalonet, http://history.buffalonet.org/1832-40.html (accessed February 20, 2017).

6. "The Juba Project's Early Blackface Minstrelsy in Britain, 1842-1852," https://minstrels.library.utoronto.ca/ (accessed April 19, 2017). The author is indebted to Cynthia M. Van Ness, director of library and archives at the Buffalo History Museum for this information.

7. "Traveling the Erie Canal, 1836," EyeWitnesstoHistory.com (accessed March 9, 2017).

8. "The Canal Boat: Nathaniel Hawthorne Travels the Erie Canal," History Matters: The U.S. Survey Course on the Web, http://historymatters.gmu.edu/d/6212/ (accessed March 9, 2017).

9. Trollope, *Domestic Manners*, 293-294.

10. Carol Sheriff, *The Artificial River: The Erie Canal and the Paradox of Progress, 1817-1862* (New York: Hill and Wang, 1996), 75-78.

11. "Contemporary Photographs from Rochester, Images of the Central Library of Rochester and Monroe County," http://www.eriecanal.org/Rochester-2.html (accessed March 4, 2017).

12. "Making it Work, the Weigh Lock," http://www.eriecanal.org/UnionCollege/The_Weigh_Lock.html (accessed March 4, 2017).

13. Sheriff, *Artificial River,* 120.

14. "Mary Campbell (Highland Mary)," https://en.wikipedia.org/wiki/Mary_Campbell_(Highland_Mary) (accessed March 31, 2018).

15. William Williams, *The Tourist's Map of the State of New York Compiled from the Latest Authorities* (Utica, NY: William Williams, 1827).

16. "Traveling the Erie Canal, 1836."

17. "The Canal Boat."

18. Sheriff, *Artificial River*, 44. See also G. F. Pyle, "The Diffusion of Cholera in the

United States in the Nineteenth Century," Geographical Analysis, 1 (1969): 59-75, doi:10.1111/j.1538-4632. 1969.tb00605.x. http://onlinelibrary.wiley.com/doi/10.1111/j.1538-4632.1969.tb00605.x/full (accessed June 5, 2017).

19. "Engineering the Erie," https://sites.google.com/site/engineeringtheerie/major-challenges-and-accomplishments/montezuma-swamp (accessed March 7, 2017).

20. "Salt Industry in Syracuse," C-Span, https://www.c-span.org/video/?328403-1/salt-industry-syracuse, September 23, 2015 (accessed March 7, 2017). See also WCNY Insight, "The Historical Events of the Salt Industry Helping put Syracuse on the Map," http://video.wcny.org/video/2365942578/ Aired January 27, 2017 (accessed March 7, 2017).

21. Sarah Kozma of the Onondaga Historical Association, e-mail message to author, March 25, 2017.

22. "The Canal Boat"

23. Lewis D. Stilwell, *Migration from Vermont* (Montpelier: Vermont Historical Society, 1948), 179.

24. Ibid., 183-184.

25. *Caledonian* (St. Johnsbury, VT), 30 October 1838.

26. William Williams, *The Tourist's Map of the State of New York: Compiled from the Latest Authorities in the Surveyor General's Office* (Utica: William Williams, 1831), 7, Library of Congress, https://www.loc.gov/resource/g3804e.ct006593/ (accessed April 4, 2018).

27. "The Canal Boat."

28. Williams, *Tourist Map of New York* (1831), 7.

29. Lionel D. Wyld, *Low Bridge! Folklore and the Erie Canal* (Syracuse: Syracuse University Press, 1962), 47.

30. Ibid., 69-74.

31. *New York Tribune*, 7 October 1841.

32. Sheriff, *Artificial River*, 72-73.

33. Ibid., 71-72.

34. Ibid., 72.

35. Ibid., 54.

36. Russell P. Bellico, *Sails and Steam in the Mountains: A Maritime and Military History of Lake George and Lake Champlain* (Fleischmanns, NY: Purple Mountain Press, 1992), 268.

CHAPTER 9

1. Tom Kelleher, *The Debit Economy of 1830s New England* (Sturbridge, MA: Old Sturbridge Village, n.d.) http://www.teachushistory.org/detocqueville-visit-united-states/articles/debit-economy-1830s-new-england (accessed April 5, 2018). See also J. C. Furnas, *The Americans: A Social History of the United States, 1587-1914* (New York: G.P. Putnam's Sons, 1969), 129-130, 245.

2. Essex, Vermont, Land Records, Volume 8, 55.

3. Fletcher, Vermont, Land Records, Volume 7, 418. Stephen F. Hopkins to Roswell B. Fay of Williston, October 21, 1847, $2,750 for 300 acres, plus another 25 acres subject to rent.

4. The 1850 Agricultural Census summary for the Brown farm shows they had 200 acres of improved land, 100 acres of unimproved land, a $3,000 cash value for the farm, and 24 milch cows. Their production included 300 bushels of Irish potatoes, 500 pounds of butter, 6,000 pounds of cheese, 50 tons of hay, and 600 pounds of maple sugar. The 1860 Agricultural Census summary listed 230 acres of improved land and 54 acres of unimproved land; the farm now had a $7,000 cash value. There were 25 milch cows, 2 oxen, and 5 sheep, together worth $1,200. The farm produced 300 bushels of Irish potatoes, 700 pounds of butter, 5,500 pounds of cheese, 75 tons of hay, 1,500 pounds of maple sugar, 150 bushels of Indian corn, 431 bushels of oats, and 1,236 pounds of hops.

5. Fletcher, Vermont, Land Records, Volume 9, 241. R. B. Fay of Williston to Reed, October 25, 1856, $4,000. Same land deeded to Fay on October 21, 1847 on which Reed lived, by Stephen F. Hopkins.

6. "Jackson Fay Brown House," http://www.bartosh.com/jfbrownhouse/ (accessed March 31, 2018).

7. Fletcher, Vermont, Land Records, Volume 10, 501. Reed and wife to Sumner Carpenter, November 26, 1866, for $9,000. Same land and premises deeded to R. B. Brown by Roswell B. Fay on October 25, 1856, as recorded in Volume 9, 241.

8. Williston, Vermont, Land Records, Volume 13, 137. March 9, 1867, purchased for $2,500.

9. Richard Allen, *North Williston: Down Depot Hill* (Charleston, NC: The History Press, 2011), 129-137.

10. Williston, Vermont, Land Records, Volume 13, 361.

11. Charles Nordhoff, "California, How to Go There, and What to See by the Way," *Harper's New Monthly Magazine*, 44 (May 1872): 865-881. Central Pacific Railroad Photographic History Museum, http://cprr.org/Museum/Nordhoff.html (accessed March 31, 2018).

12. Lucia Darling, *Diaries, 1858 to 1914*, Williston Historical Society Collection, Dorothy Alling Memorial Library, Williston, Vermont.

13. *Walton's Vermont Register, Farmers' Almanac and Business Directory for 1886* (White River Junction, VT: White River Paper Company, 1886)

14. Hamilton Child, ed., *Gazetteer and Business Directory of Chittenden County, 1882-83* (Syracuse: Journal Office, 1882), 256.

15. Allen, *North Williston*, 49.

16. Henry M. Seely, *Fifth Report of the Vermont Board of Agriculture for the Year 1878* (Montpelier, VT: J. and J. M. Poland, 1878), 175.

17. Child, *Gazetteer of Chittenden County, 1882-83*, 531.

18. Paul Wood, e-mail message to author, February 6, 2016.

19. *Burlington Weekly Free Press*, 25 September 1874, 15 September 1876.

20. There is some contradictory information on Reed Brown's birth date. According to Vermont Vital Records, with this death date, his birth date would have been on or about July 5, 1810. His gravestone confirms the date of death, but notes a different birth date, June 11, 1810.

21. Hiram Phelps, *Journal*, Williston Historical Society Collection, Dorothy Alling Memorial Library, Williston, Vermont, 152, 158.

22. Richmond, Vermont, Land Records, Volume 6, 159.

23. Jan Albers, *Hands on the Land: A History of the Vermont Landscape* (Cambridge, MA: MIT Press, 2000), 173.

24. *The United States District Court for the District of Vermont, Bankruptcy Act of 1841 Case Files, Case No. 997, Nathaniel Brown*. National Archives and Records Administration, 400 West Pershing Road, Kansas City, Missouri 64108.

25. Hinesburgh, Vermont, Land Records, Volume 13, 233-234. March 27, 1851.

26. Hinesburgh, Vermont, Land Records, Volume 13, 436. On August 17, 1852, Nathaniel and Melinda transferred to Dow for $600 a village lot, blacksmith shop, and a dwelling at the north end of the village. This was the same land William C. Benton (and Lucretia) deeded to Nathaniel and Dow in the spring of 1851.

27. Ancestry.com, *1860 United States Federal Census* [database online].

28. *Williston, Vermont Index to Cemetery Burials and Death Records, 1786-2001*. Williston Cemetery Commission, 2002.

29. Richmond cemetery records do not reveal burial documentation for Melinda. Her death date is confirmed in *Index to Births, Marriages, and Deaths* for Richmond. For Oscar: Ancestry.com, *Vermont, Vital Records*, 1720-1908 [database online].

30. Ancestry.com, *1880 United States Federal Census* [database online]. Ancestry.com, *Michigan, Death Records, 1867-1950* [database online].

$\mathscr{S}$ELECTED BIBLIOGRAPHY

PRIMARY SOURCES

Brown, Reed B. *Reed B. Brown Journal*. Williston Historical Society, Williston, Vermont.

Darling, Lucia. *Lucia Darling Diaries, 1858 to 1914*. Williston Historical Society, Williston, Vermont.

Phelps, Hiram. *Hiram Phelps Journal*. Williston Historical Society, Williston, Vermont.

The United States District Court for the District of Vermont, Bankruptcy Act of 1841 Case Files, Case No. 997, Nathaniel Brown. National Archives and Records Administration, 400 West Pershing Road, Kansas City, Missouri 64108.

Webster, Daniel. *Domestic Letters, 1784-1906*. Department of State, RG 59: https://catalog.archives.gov/id/29730448.

SECONDARY SOURCES

Albers, Jan. *Hands on the Land*. Cambridge, MA: The M.I.T. Press, 2000.

Aldrich, Mark. *Death Rode the Rails: American Railroad Accidents and Safety, 1828-1965*. Baltimore: Johns Hopkins University Press, 2006.

Allen, Richard. *North Williston: Down Depot Hill*. Charleston, SC: The History Press, 2011.

Anbinder, Tyler. *Five Points: The 19th-Century New York City Neighborhood That Invented Tap Dance, Stole Elections, and Became the World's Most Notorious Slum*. New York: The Free Press, 2001.

Barber, John W. and Henry Howe. *Historical Collections of the State of New York*. New York: S. Tuttle, 1846.

Bellico, Russell P. *Sails and Steam in the Mountains: A Maritime and Military History of Lake George and Lake Champlain*. Fleischmanns, NY: Purple Mountain Press, 1992.

Bernstein, Peter L. *Wedding of the Waters: The Erie Canal and the Making of a Great Nation*. New York: W. W. Norton & Company, 2005.

Boucher, John N. *History of Westmoreland County, Pennsylvania*. New York: Lewis Publishing Company, 1906.

Burrows, Edwin G. and Mike Wallace. *Gotham: A History of New York City to 1898*. New York: Oxford University Press, 1999.

Child, Hamilton, ed. *Gazetteer and Business Directory of Chittenden County, Vermont, 1882-83*. Syracuse: Journal Office, 1882.

Dickens, Charles. *American Notes*. 1842, London: Penguin Books, 2004.

Dobyns, Kenneth W. *The Patent Office Pony: A History of the Early Patent Office*. Kenneth W. Dobyns, 1994.

Doyle, William B. *Centennial History of Summit County, Ohio and Representative Citizens*. Chicago: Biographical Publishing Company, 1908.

Ellsworth, Henry L. *A Digest of Patents Issued by the United States, Including the Years 1839, 1840, 1841*. Washington, D.C.: William Greer, 1842.

Federal Writers' Project of the Works Progress Administration for the State of New Jersey. *New Jersey: A Guide to its Present and Past*. New York: Hastings House, 1939.

Furnas J. C. *The Americans: A Social History of the United States, 1587-1914*. New York: G. P. Putnam's Sons, 1969.

Gieck, Jack. *Early Akron's Industrial Valley: A History of Cascade Locks*. Kent, OH: The Kent State University Press, 2008.

Gregory, Thomas G., Christina M. McVay, and Dennis R. Sutton. *Ravenna: A Bicentennial Album of Nineteenth-Century Photographs*. Ravenna, OH: Portage County Historical Society, 1999.

Grismer, Karl H. *Akron and Summit County*. Akron, OH: Summit County Historical Society, 1952.

Guyette, Elise A. *Discovering Black Vermont: African American Farmers in Hinesburgh, 1790-1890*. Lebanon, NH: University Press of New England, 2010.

Hart, J. Percy. *Hart's History and Directory of the Three Towns, Brownsville, Bridgeport, West Brownsville, Also Abridged History of Fayette County & Western Pennsylvania*. Cadwallader, PA: J. P. Hart, 1904.

Hill, Ralph N. *Lake Champlain: Key to Liberty*. Montpelier, VT: Vermont Life Magazine, 1976.

Howe, Daniel W. *What Hath God Wrought: The Transformation of America, 1815-1848*. New York: Oxford University Press, 2007.

Hunter, Alfred. *A Popular Catalogue of the Extraordinary Curiosities in the National Institute Arranged in the Building Belonging to the Patent Office*. Washington, D.C.: Alfred Hunter, 1855.

Knepper, George W. *Ohio and Its People*. Kent, OH: Kent State University Press, 2003.

Lane, Samuel A. *Fifty Years and Over of Akron and Summit County*. Akron, OH: Beacon Job Department, 1892.

Lewis, Tom. *Washington: A History of Our National City*. New York: Basic Books, 2015.

Nicklin, Philip. *Journey Through Pennsylvania, 1835, by Canal, Rail, and Stage Coach*. Philadelphia: Grigg and Elliot, 1836.

Olin, Oscar E. *Akron and Environs: Historical, Biographical, Genealogical*. Chicago: Lewis Publishing Company, 1917.

Perrin, William H. *History of Summit County with an Outline Sketch of Ohio*. Chicago: Baskins & Battey, Historical Publishers, 1881.

Philbrick, Nathaniel. *Sea of Glory: America's Voyage of Discovery, The U.S. Exploring Expedition, 1838-1842*. New York: Penguin Group, 2003.

Price, Mark J. *Lost Akron*. Charleston, SC: The History Press, 2015.

Reed, Robert C. *Train Wrecks: A Pictorial History of Accidents on The Main Line*. Seattle: Superior Publishing Company, 1968.

Riggs, Harriet W. et. al. *Richmond, Vermont: A History of More Than 200 Years*. Burlington, VT: Queen City Printers, 2007.

Rose, Albert C. *Historic American Roads: From Frontier Trails to Superhighways*. New York: Crown Publishers, Inc., 1976.

Ross, Ogden. *The Steamboats of Lake Champlain, 1809 to 1930*. Rutland, VT: Vermont Heritage Press, 1997.

Schama, Simon. *The American Future: A History*. New York: HarperCollins Publishers, 2009.

Sheriff, Carol. *The Artificial River: The Erie Canal and the Paradox of Progress, 1817-1862*. New York: Hill and Wang, 1996.

Sherman, Michael, Gene Sessions, and P. Jeffrey Potash. *Freedom and Unity: A History of Vermont*. Barre, VT: Vermont Historical Society, 2004.

Stilwell, Lewis D. *Migration from Vermont*. Montpelier, VT: Vermont Historical Society, 1948.

Trollope, Frances M. *Domestic Manners of the Americans*. London: Whittaker, Treacher, & Co., 1832.

Viola, Herman J. and Carolyn Margolis, eds. *Magnificent Voyagers: The U.S. Exploring Expedition, 1838-1842*. Washington, D.C.: Smithsonian Institution Press, 1985.

Wyld, Lionel D. *Low Bridge!: Folklore and the Erie Canal*. Syracuse: Syracuse University Press, 1962.

PERIODICALS

Buffalo Whig and Journal (NY)

Burlington Free Press (VT)

Burlington Weekly Free Press (VT)

Caledonian (St. Johnsbury, VT)

Fort Bragg Advocate (CA)

Geauga Republican (Bostwick, OH)

Green-Mountain Freeman (Montpelier, VT)

Harper's New Monthly Magazine

Klondike Sun (Dawson City, Canada)

Maumee City Express (OH)

Morning Herald (New York City)

New York Tribune

Pittsburgh Gazette

Pilot and Transcript (Baltimore)

Polynesian (Honolulu)

Portage County Democrat (Ravenna, OH)

Portage Sentinel (Ravenna, OH)

Summit County Beacon (Akron, OH)

Vermont Telegraph (Brandon)

Washingtonian (Washington, D.C.)

Weekly Graphic (Kirksville, MO)

MAPS, DIRECTORIES, AND GUIDES

Elliot, William. *The Washington Guide*. Washington: Franck Taylor, 1837.

Graham, C. W. *Crary's Directory for the City of Buffalo*. Buffalo: Faxon & Graves, 1841.

Greene, Asa. *A Glance at New York*. New York: Asa Greene, 1837.

Harris, Isaac. *Harris' General Business Directory of the Cities of Pittsburgh and Allegheny*. Pittsburgh: A. A. Anderson, 1841.

Holley, O. L. *A Description of the City of New York*. New York: J. Disturnell, 1847.

Hunter, Alfred. *A Popular Catalogue of the Extraordinary Curiosities in the National Institute Arranged in the Building Belonging to the Patent Office*. Washington, D. C.: Alfred Hunter, 1855.

___. *The Washington and Georgetown Directory, Strangers' Guide Book for Washington*. Washington, D.C.: Kirkwood & McGill, 1853.

Keim, De Benneville Randolph. *Keim's Illustrated Guide to the Museum of Models, Patent Office*. Washington, D. C.: De B. Randolph Keim, 1874.

Mac Cabe, Julius P. B. *First Directory of Cleveland and Ohio City*. Cleveland: Sanford & Lott, 1837.

Peet, Elijah. *Peet's General Business Directory of the Cities of Cleveland and Ohio, 1846-47*. Sanford & Hayword, 1845.

Ruggles, Edward. *Picture of New-York in 1846*. New York: Homans & Ellis, 1846.

Walker, H. N. *Buffalo City Directory*. Buffalo: Steele's Press, 1842.

Walton, Ezekiel. *Walton's Vermont Register, Farmers' Almanac and Business Directory for 1886*. White River Jct., VT: White River Paper Company, 1886.

Williams, William. *Tourist's Map of the State of New York*. Utica, NY: William Williams, 1827.

___. *The Tourist's Map of the State of New York: Compiled from the Latest Authorities in the Surveyor General's Office*. Utica, NY: William Williams, 1831.

___. *The Traveller's Pocket Map of New York: From the Best Authorities*. Utica, NY: William Williams, 1826.

$\mathscr{I}$NDEX

The author at Schoharie Crossing, a New York State Historic Site.

BOUT THE AUTHOR

Richard H. Allen is a native of Plattsburgh, New York and has lived in Vermont since 1973. He received his B.A. from Harpur College, State University of New York at Binghamton, and his M.Ed. from the University of North Dakota. He taught elementary school for 40 years, 37 of those years in Williston, Vermont. He lives with his wife Lucille in Essex and they have three grown children. He has authored or co-authored six other books: *The Vermont Geography Book; The History of Williston Central School, 1950-2000; Essex and Essex Junction*, with Lucille; *North Williston: Down Depot Hill; Williston, Vermont: Commemorating 250 Years of Town History;* and *Ambition & Grit: The Life of Truman Naramore, Civil War Veteran and Entrepreneur.*

CPSIA information can be obtained
at www.ICGtesting.com
Printed in the USA
LVHW050906250420
654389LV00005B/394